DIARIES NOTEBOOKS + SKETCHBOOKS

D1470761

ESSAYS

#1. Dr. Stephen Bury
Notebook as relay
"I AM FOR THE ART OF FAT TRUCK-TIRES AND BLACK EYES"
P. 200

#2. Stefan Sagmeister
'MY YEAR WITHOUT CLIENTS'
p 204

GRAPHIC IS DISTRIBUTED BY:

AUSTRALIA:
Tower Books
Unit 2, 17 Rodborough Road
Frenchs Forest, NSW 2086
T +62 2 9975 5566
F +62 2 9975 5599
info@towerbooks.com.au
www.towerbooks.com.au

BELGIUM:
Bookstores
Exhibitions International
Kol. Begaultlaan 17
B-3012 Leuven
T +32 16 296 900
F +32 16 296 129
orders@exhibitionsinternational.be
www.exhibitionsinternational.be

CHINA, HONG KONG:
Foreign Press Distributors Ltd
Room 6, Ground Floor, Block B
Proficient Industrial Center
6 Wang Kwun Road
T +852 2756 8193
F +852 2799 8840

FRANCE:
Critique Livres Distribution SAS
BP 93-24 rue Malmaison
93172 Bagnolet Cedex
T +33 1 4360 3910
F +33 1 4897 3706
critiques.livres@wanadoo.fr

GERMANY, AUSTRIA, SWITZERLAND:
Distribution/Auslieferung
Bookstores
BUGRIM Verlagsauslieferung
Saalburgstrasse 3
D-12099 Berlin
Germany
T +49 30 6068457
F +49 30 6063476
bugrim@bugrim.de
www.bugrim.de

Newsstands
IPS Pressevertrieb GmbH
Carl-Zeiss-Strasse 5
D-53340 Meckenheim
T +49 22 258801 122
F +49 22 258801 199
publishing@ips-pressevertrieb.de
www.ips-pressevertrieb.de

INDONESIA:
Aksara
Jalan Kemang Raya 8b
Jakarta 12730
T +62 21 7199 288
F +62 21 7199 282
info@aksara.com
www.aksara.com

ITALY:
Happy Books SRL
Via Grandi 159
41100 Modena
T +39 059 454 219
F +39 059 450 343
happy@happybooks.it

Idea srl
Via Lago Transimeno, 23/2 (ZI)
36015 Schio (VI)
T +39 455 576 574
F +39 445 577 764
info@ideabooks.it
www.ideabooks.it

LIBRIMPORT SAS
Via Biondelli 9
20141 Milano
T +39 2 8950 1422
F +39 2 8950 2811
librimport@libero.it

Red Edizioni Sas
Viale Prampolini 110
41100 Modena
T +39 59 212 792
F +39 59 4392 133
info@redonline.it

JAPAN:
Shimada Yosho
TPlace, 5-5-25, Minami-Aoyama,
Minato-Ku
Tokyo, 107-0062
T +81 3 3407 3937
F +81 3 3407 0989
sales@shimada.attnet.ne.jp

KOREA:
Beatboy Inc.
Kangnam-Ku Shinsa-Dong 666-11
Baegang Building 135-897
Seoul
T +82 2 3444 8367
F +82 2 541 8358
yourbeatboy@hanmail.net

MALAYSIA:
How & Why Sdn Bhd
101A, Jalan SS2/24
47300 Petaling Jaya
Selangor
T +60 3 7877 4800
F +60 3 7877 4600
E: info@howwwhy.com
www.howwwhy.com

MEXICO:
Books VIP, S.A. de C.V.
Andrés Molina Enríquez # 480 Casa B
col Reforma Iztaccíhuatl CP 08810
Del Iztacalco, México DF; MÉXICO
T +52 55 3330 4830
F +52 55 3330 4831
booksvip@yahoo.com.mx
www.booksvip.com

THE NETHERLANDS:
Bookstores
Betapress BV
Burg. Krollaan 14
5126 PT Gilze
T +31 161 457 800
F +31 161 457 224

Other
BIS Publishers
Herengracht 370-372
1016 CH Amsterdam
T +31 20 524 7560
F +31 20 524 7557
bis@bispublishers.nl
www.bispublishers.nl

RUSSIA:
Design Books Ltd
14 office, 3 block,
20, Pyatnitskaya street,
115184 Moscow, Russia.
T +7 095 959 5397
F +7 095 959 5397

SINGAPORE:
Basheer Graphic Books
Block 231, Bain Street
#04-19 Bras Basah Complex
180231 Singapore
T +65 336 0810
F +65 334 1950

Page One Pte Ltd
20 Kaki Bukit View
Kaki Bukit Techpark II
415956 Singapore
T +65 6742 2088
F +65 6744 2088
enquiries@pageonebookshop.com

SPAIN:
ACTAR
Roca i Batlle 2 i 4
08023 Barcelona
T +34 93 418 77 59
F +34 93 418 67 07
info@actar-mail.com
www.actar.es

TAIWAN:
Long Sea International Book Co. Ltd.
1/F No. 204 Si Wei Rd
Taipei 106 Taiwan ROC
T +886 2 2706 6838
F +886 2 2706 6109
thfang@ms16.hinet.net
www.longsea.co.tw

TURKEY:
Evrensel Grafikir Yayincilik
Gulbahar Mahl
Gayret SK No:11
80300-01 Mecidiyekoy/Istanbul
T +90 212 356 7276
F +90 212 356 7278
evrensely@superonline.com

UNITED KINGDOM:
Bookstores
Publisher Group UK
8 The Arena
Mollison Avenue
Enfield
Middlesex EN3 7NL
T +44 20 8804 0400
F +44 20 8804 0044
info@pguk.co.uk

Other
Comag Specialist
Tavistock Works
Tavistock Road
West Drayton
Middlesex UB7 7QX
T +44 1895 433 800
F +44 1895 433 801
andy.hounslow@comag.co.uk

USA/CANADA
Lords News International, inc.
651 Observer Highway
Hoboken, NJ 07030
T +1 201 798 2555
F +1 201 798 5335
support@lordsnewsinternational.com
www.lordsusa.com

All other countries
BIS Publishers
Herengracht 370-372
1016 CH AMSTERDAM
T +31 20 524 7560
F +31 20 524 7557
bis@bispublishers.nl
www.bispublishers.nl

**GRAPHIC MAGAZINE
ISSUE TEN**

EDITORS
Marc-A Valli
Editor-in-Chief
marc@magmabooks.com

Richard Brereton
Features Editor
graphic@magmabooks.com

Mairi Duthie
Matt Willey
Zoë Bather

DESIGN
Studio8 design
www.studio8design.co.uk

PUBLISHER
Rudolf van Wezel

PRODUCTION
Rietje van Vreden

PRINTING
D2Print Pte Ltd

EDITORIAL OFFICE
Graphic Magazine
c/o Magma
117–119 Clerkenwell Road
London EC1R 5BY
United Kingdom
T +44 20 7242 9522
F +44 20 7242 9504
graphic@magmabooks.com
www.magmabooks.com

**PUBLISHING AND
ADVERTISING**
BIS Publishers
Herengracht 370–372
NL-1016 CH Amsterdam
The Netherlands
T +31 20 524 75 60
F +31 20 524 75 57
graphic@bispublishers.nl
www.bispublishers.nl

A BIS Publishers publication

ISBN 90-6369-147-5

Copyright © 2006
BIS Publishers Amsterdam, the Netherlands

SUBSCRIPTIONS:
Bruil & van de Staaij
PO Box 75
7940 AB Meppel
The Netherlands
T +31 522 261 303
F +31 522 257 827
info@bruil.info
www.bruil.info

SUBSCRIPTION RATES:
Subscription 1 year (2 issues)
including VAT and airmail:
The Netherlands: €40
Europe: €45
Other countries: $61

Student subscriptions: 20% discount
(only valid with a copy of your student registration form)

TARN-ATION

An interview with **Jonathan Caouette** by **Richard Brereton**

Tarnation – a hybrid word derived from 'tarnished' and 'eternal damnation' – is the name of Jonathan Caouette's critically acclaimed documentary about his mother Renee Le Blanc's long struggle with mental illness. It is also a coming-of-age story, telling of his upbringing in a 1970s Houston suburb.

Caouette's mother was a child model who was later paralyzed for six months after falling from a garage roof. After the accident she suffered from depression – the electric shock treatment she was prescribed only made matters worse.

From the day of his birth, Caouette watched his mother's constant struggle with mental illness and saw her life dragged through the revolving doors of countless mental health institutions. He witnessed his mother's rape, stumbled through foster care and was eventually adopted by his maternal grandparents Adolph and Rosemary Davis.

Using old home movies, tape recordings, photographs, clippings and interviews, Caouette pieced together the traumatic episodes of his life into a compelling account of a son's unwavering love for his mother.

The film begins in present day New York, with Caouette talking to his mother's doctors after she survived an accidental lithium overdose.

I started my interview with Jonathan Caouette by asking him whether he found it difficult to talk about such a personal film.

JC: I've come to a place where I don't want to say I'm desensitized or detached necessarily, but I think I was in a place initially where at Sundance I was knocked-kneed. I couldn't get the words out edgewise, so I quickly constructed these canned answers as a way to create a defence mechanism. I started getting so bored of saying the same things over and over again that I now try and talk without repeating myself. And through that process I've become ok with it. It's been an emotional rollercoaster.

RB: Tarnation begins in the present day with footage of your mother singing 'Let it Shine'. We immediately know that your mother has severe mental health issues. We then see you on the phone talking with doctors about your mother, who has just had a lithium overdose. When did you decide to make the film? What prompted that decision?

Prior to my mother having the overdose, I'd been working on the film sequentially for six months. I had thirty-five minutes and was wondering what to do next. I was sort of paralyzed. I didn't want to put this out to heal myself, or be that personal. I really wanted to work with the footage on a more experimental creative level: to put the footage out there under the safety constraints, but leave it ambiguous to the viewer as to what they were watching, and what the footage meant.

So I wrote this screenplay which was really ironic because it was about my mother living with me in New York, before I even brought her back to live with me in New York. I just did it as a sort of exercise, like an elongated *Twighlight Zone* episode.

It was about someone going into psychiatric hospital, using flashback sequences. One of the protagonists was going to be someone else playing me. At one point he goes into psychiatric hospital, brings a video tape with him and shows one of the doctors a montage of me imitating my mother when I was eleven. I wanted to used the footage in completely different way. That was one idea, using fictitious people with bits of me as a child. A sort of power-psychological, elongated *Twighlight Zone* thing, loosely structured on a hyper-paranoid Ira Levin novel from the seventies. It was even going to talk about the notion of my mother's mental illness by way of some supernatural occurrence, a shape-shifting thing that had happened.

I wrote two screenplays, and as soon as I wrote them I succumbed to the fact that the footage I had and the screenplay were two different entities. Something pulled me towards going after just the footage on its own.

So using an iMac, I created a thirty-five minute opening to the film that started with a Nick Drake song. My first idea was to lay down a soundtrack and use text to evoke a story, like the use of music in Von Trier's *Breaking the Waves*.

So using iMac instead of going to an editing suite enabled you to edit and play with what you had?

Yeah, in my own time. Then I had to fly back to Texas. I'd found out that my grandfather, because of his early signs of Alzheimer's and dementia from having a haematoma due to a bad car accident, was inadvertently allowing my mother to overdose on lithium. He hadn't realized she was literally dying in front of his eyes.

In Texas I continued to document some of the stuff that was going on. I didn't document the actual overdose. The scene you see in the film is not actually a result of my mother overdosing on lithium, that scene was actually shot two years prior when she was having a really bad bout of mania. When she overdosed on lithium she was in an intensive care unit and couldn't walk or talk for about six months. There was just no way in hell I was going to pick the camera up and document all of that.

When your mother says, "Speak your truth. Even the dull and ignorant have their story to tell", whose words is she speaking?

That's from a famous poem, 'The Desiderata'. It's from 1970s affirmation poster.

A Tony Robbins-type thing?

Yeah, something like that. I remember her having this poster, one of those seventies posters with the landscape on it, a river and this beautiful poem. The audio, the poem, the nursery rhymes, the banter between my mother and grandmother, was on an audio tape recorded in 1975 which I found behind the washer and dryer when I was about 10 or 11 and I'd held onto it. So inevitably that went into *Tarnation*.

Had you seen photos and home footage used in other films?

Yeah, I know people have done this a lot, even before, the first thing that I saw, that I was aware of were, Derek Jarman and Gus Van Sant. I like the way Gus Van Sant had used super 8 footage to evoke memory in *Drugstore Cowboy*, *My Private Idaho*, and around that time I saw *The Last of England*, which was done on super 8 or at least felt like super 8. Now that we're moving in the high definition world it's a cliché to even think about super 8 because it has been overdone. Even though I'd love to make an entire movie on super 8 one day. When I saw Harmony Korine's *Gummo*, I just felt it was someone imitating the world I knew all too well: wow, there's this wonderfully talented filmmaker who put this out, maybe I can do something similar. He'd set a precedent for something.

When you were young your mother took you from Texas to Chicago, where she was raped upon arrival. Did you witness the assault?

Yeah, I was four, and I remember us getting into our car in the dead of winter with this guy and his family. I sort of remember, like snippets in film, when we were in a hotel room, a big white hotel room. I remember hiding under the bed as it was happening. It wasn't quite clear at the time, but I heard it, and I remember hearing about it for the rest of my life. Always spoken about openly with my family. I had a pretty bizarre family: nothing was ever edited in a conversation, nothing that you would normally keep from a child.

Following the rape you were placed into care?

I was in a foster home in Marion, Illinois for a while. Came back to Texas briefly, but my mum was really sick at that point. People in Texas are very nosey and aware – they don't have a lot to do, and so they tend to be very involved in other people's business, particularly where I grew up in Houston. The whole neighbourhood knew about our crazy family at that point. And as soon as I got back from Chicago, an incident happened with my mum: she broke out one of the neighbour's windows. All kinds of things happened. I think I remember going to a neighbour's home smelling of gasoline. Eventually the neighbours banded together to call child protection services.

My grandmother had gone into hospital to have a hysterectomy and the recovery process wasn't going very well, so she had to heal at her sister's house and grandfather had to work all day and my mother had gone into hospital about a week after coming back from Chicago. Child Protection Services picked me up and put me into a foster home for quite a while. It was during a period when I had forgotten about my family. When you are that young your memory and your ideas, your interpretation of space and time is all just so different to when you're nine or ten.

The foster home experience was really, really traumatic in a lot of ways. It branded itself into my psyche. I always wanted to do a movie about it, and on some levels, I suppose I have.

Your mother and father never being around, how did their absence impact you? How did it impact on your mental well-being?

Immensely. When I became older and began to formulate my own opinions about the world around me – comparing and contrasting my life to those of other kids lives – of course there was a huge sense of loneliness and abandonment. At the age of six I was already aware that my life was – and was going to continue to be – substantially different from that of most peoples. I just knew things were different and I was probably bound for a real ride.

In one scene in the film – set around 1981, you were perhaps only ten or eleven year old – we see you portraying a grown-up women in a very bad adult relationship. What was that footage?

I used what I knew and what I knew I could pull off. I'd acquired a video camera from my big brother. I was in a big brother and big sister program, a mentor program for kids who were fatherless or from dysfunctional families.

You later said: 'Life's one big long trip. Nobody is supposed to know I'm gay. I'm not crazy. I'm just stupid.' It made me think how mature you were. Do you think that because of what you experienced so early in your life, you matured faster than other kids?

I think so. I used to really frighten the other kids in my

neighbourhood. It's strange, there was a kind of acquired aesthetic that I had, about art, the world, New York, culture, film and Andy Warhol. I don't necessarily know where it came from. I don't mean to be narcissistic, but I really think as a child I was a little ahead of things on some levels. I had just seen so much stuff up to that point. Kids are really good mimics – that's been really apparent with my ten year old son Josh.

I imagine he's got you down?

He's got me down. He can do a really amazing British accent in a way most adult couldn't. It's something torn from the same cloth, how kids can learn multitudes of languages at an early age. They have no inhibitions, they just absorb things. And kids react to what they know.

When you were a teenager your grandparents took the decision to have you hospitalised for acting out. How did that impact on your relationship with them? How did you see psychiatrists, shrinks, councillors, those types of people?

Because of the circumstances in which I was introduced to psychiatrists and social workers, they became these people that I felt I needed to fear. Because of that I was always on my best behaviour with anyone outside of my family. Inside the house, on the other hand, because of the chaos and because I couldn't trust what was going on all of the time, I reacted, bust holes in the wall, threw furniture, pulled the Venetian blinds down, I was just an angry, out-of-control kid. I was reacting to the given circumstance, which was uncertainty, a fear of being lied to.

Lied to by whom?

My grandparents, saying one thing, then turning around and completely contradicting what they were saying. Chaos. Absolute fucking chaos. Looking back I don't know, I wouldn't change a thing about my family. I wouldn't want my mother or my grandparents to be anything else.

Your mother and Liz Taylor! She clearly loved Liz Taylor.

She had been told she looked like Elizabeth Taylor, and which I have to agree with, did and does. I think something that she took and ran with, and always made reference to. The whole notion of Elizabeth Taylor was completely branded into my psyche by the time I was ten.

Carrie (1976) and The Exorcist (1973) are both movies you used to quote lines from. Why?

I'd seen both films probably when I was about 10 years old. There was something about Sissy Spacek's naivety and something about something entering someone's body in The Exorcist that resonated. Whenever my mum had gotten sick it just reminded me of someone being possessed by something. The whole scapegoat-ism of Sissy Spacek's character really did something…

People will never make movies like they did then. They've established a formula right now – back then people were still finding the formula, there were just these wonderfully mesmerizing atmospheric qualities with the restrained lack of editing. *Let's Scare Jessica to Death* (1971), is a great film I loved, a really fantastic horror film about a woman comes out of a psychiatric hospital and becomes a vampire.

There's one moment in the film when your mother says: 'You won't have a family when I die.' You reply: 'That ain't true.' She replies: 'It is true.' That must be hard to hear. It was clear it was not said in malice, but still hard to hear. Who was there to comfort you?

I suppose the obvious one is David, who I've been together with for nine years now. Interestingly enough, there was alternate ending to the film where my grandfather is talking about an angel coming to heal you and all that. I thought that the story that my grandfather had told me all my life, which I happened to catch in an interview, was some sort of Jewish folklore that maybe his father had told him about. Then pretty recently I realized it was in the movie *Key Largo* (1948). But I loved the idea of that story so much that I wanted their pay-off, so in the original cut of the film my grandfather actually pulls out a gun and shoots me and the camera drops. Another device lending a certain ambiguity as to what you are seeing is that the filmmaker's brain is dying: it goes into this heavenly esoteric place where it's just me and David and a white ethereal world and we're both naked and he's wearing angel wings…

That was a fantasy version?

[Laughs] Yeah, the two-hour cut of the film that premiered in New

York is actually pretty cool. I have to admit I loved that scene but I decided to leave the film on one plane of reality. I took that last scene and augmented it in the centre of the film and it now serves as David healing me in a sense, in order to enable me to have enough strength for me to heal my mum.

And before David was around? Who was around in your teenage years to provide that role?

A women by the name of Joan Williams, who is actually the mother of my son. She's not in the film. But if I ever do sequel or an equal I have no doubt she will be in the film.

When you met your father for the first time in a very long time your mother also happened to be in New York. She jokes: 'I'm Dolly Parton's little sister. Daddy says I'm a cowgirl." You all seemed so relaxed. Didn't you feel resentment or frustration towards your father for Never being there?

Absolutely, that's why it was a quasi re-enactment. In reality I'd met my father when I was 19, but because I only had footage of meeting him again when I was 30, I used that.

The few times my father has appeared have always been very awkward. He claims he didn't know I existed when I originally contact him. The way he left my mother and me, and some of the things he talked to me about in the first five minutes of me contacting him on the phone were in the film. He's a seriously loose cannon. I had to go back and candy-coat a lot of the footage in order for him sign off and be in the film. Within the first five minutes of the conversation he said: 'You sound gay. Are you gay? Well you don't have AIDS do you? Cause if you have AIDS. I don't want anything to do with you.' Then preceded to tell me my crazy mother – quote – was just 'a good piece of ass'. He's a total nut job, a hick from New Hampshire. I found out I was a love child, he was a door-to-door salesman and they got married two weeks later. It was the early seventies and he left my mom six months later. My mother claims he knew she was pregnant, but I don't know what the truth is.

Does that suggest you and him are somewhat remote?

Yes. We're worlds away.

You say in the film, 'I don't want to turn out like my mother!' Are you afraid that, because of so much trauma, this might be a genuine fear?

Not necessarily. I'm a pretty depressed person myself. I wouldn't say miserable, but I'm depressed in the sense that it's actually transformed into a real, physical thing. I'm very fatigued and I long for the energy that I once used to have in my formative years, but a lot of that fatigue of course comes from all the responsibility I have had to endure. Just extreme responsibility. I have this balancing act that I have to endure: right now I am playing social worker, trying to get my mother into an assisted living program in the New York area, and my grandfather is living with us in New York. It's been exhausting to an extent I cannot even begin to describe.

I can only imagine. I don't suppose you made masses of money from Tarnation yet?

No, it wasn't very profitable. But as of August 8th there will be a big monkey lifted off my shoulder. If all the stars fall into place mother will be going into this place upstate – sort of a residential assisted living, not a hospital, a slightly controlled atmosphere where they do medication management.

My last question was really: is life still a struggle? Or did the film set you free?

I live this sequel every day, and it's a never-ending situation. I'm living with it. This is how it is.

I found Tarnation compelling in many ways because your depiction of your mother's mental health was so understanding.

I've never wanted to slap a label on anything, I honestly think 'mentally ill' people are just surviving. In a fucked-up world, who is to say that these people aren't actually accessing something we can't see?

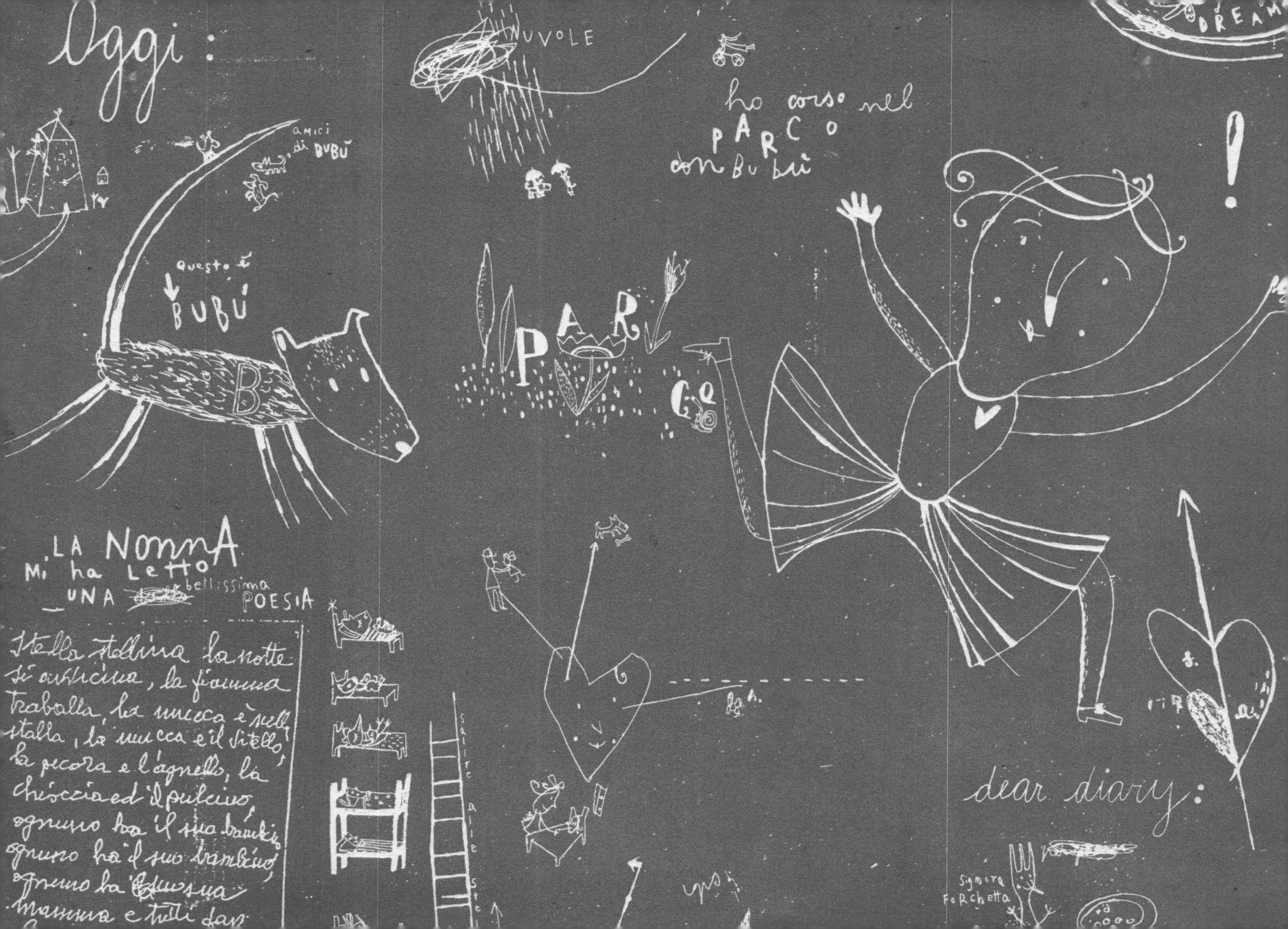

DREAM

dear diary

Signora Forchetta

Oggi:

ho corso nel PARCO con Bubù

NUVOLE

PARCO

amici di Bubù

Questo è BUBÙ

LA NONNA
Mi ha letto
UNA bellissima POESIA

Stella stellina la notte
si avvicina, la fiamma
traballa, la mucca è nella
stalla, la mucca ed il vitello,
la pecora e l'agnello, la
chioccia ed il pulcino
ognuno ha il suo bambino,
ognuno ha il suo bambino,
mamma ha la bambina,
mamma e tutti fan...

THE PERFECT WORKING HOLIDAY

Mairi Duthie talks to illustrator **Sara Fanelli** about her groundbreaking book *Dear Diary*

In the perfect version of a working holiday, the illustrator Sara Fanelli would pack a suitcase with paper samples, images, clippings, various bits of ephemera and found objects for collage, and head off to Florence, where she would spend the summer with her family while putting together her books; a wonderful mixture of collage, illustration and quotation. We met in the less exotic surroundings of Belsize Park to talk about her book *Dear Diary*.

Italian journals with poems and delicate drawings by her 93-year-old grandmother gave the initial inspiration for Sara's artistic exploration of the world of the diarist. She incorporated the 'expressive and beautiful' content directly into an etching – placing a panel of the meticulous, if slightly shaky handwriting of her ancestor in a bold red etching, showing a girl playing in the park with her dog.

'At the same time, I remembered being slightly naughty when I was a child, reading my sister's diary,' Sara says, leafing through a pile of sketchbooks and papers in her airy studio. 'I had collected some lovely old labels and stationery and I wanted to marry the aesthetic of these materials for handwriting and the different types of handwriting we have with a story, and show what the diaries reveal about the characters and what happened. The main idea was this: to marry the aesthetic with the story'

Sara's own style of illustration is a fairy-tale mixture of real elements, collage and drawing, perfectly suited to creating diaries where, as she explains, 'the combination of letters and images and the relationship between images and words create both the main narrative and characters, but also sub-narratives which might not be vital for the unfolding of the main story but add life to the page and picture.'

Sara moved to her sketchbooks to develop the idea of 'diaries, characters and their stories.' A flood of characters wanted to tell their stories. She lists these with affection, as if describing a gathering of close friends and relations: 'a firefly, a butterfly, a dog called BuBu, a girl called Lucy, a spider caterpillar, snail, grasshopper and an airplane. Each plays a part in the build-up to a party over the space of one day (with a small twist at the end that brings together animal and human worlds). The sketchpads helped both to develop each character and storyline down to each page. To find a structure for the book, I find the mini page-plan helps. It defines a realistic amount of content. This method also helped me to clarify the links between the characters in the story.'

Defining the structure meant that some of the cast of characters had to be dropped at this stage. The butterfly left to have a book of her own (*First Flight*, Jonathan Cape, 2002). I was happy about that and so was she.'

The remaining characters were Lucy, Chair, Spider, Firefly, Knife and Fork, Bubu and Ladybird. They each have their own section of the book, and narrate the events of the day in their own handwriting, to emphasise their personality. They also each have a brief quotation on their opening page that gives an added insight. In a separate sketchpad Fanelli made a colour palette for each character.

'These colours arose from the stationery I collected. The different papers with their lines for guiding writing give quite a distinctive graphic background, even though my characters are not conforming to the grids. The chair, for example, is very square, and it's writing is square. The background

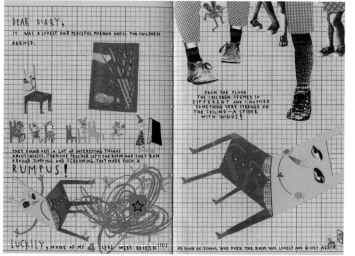

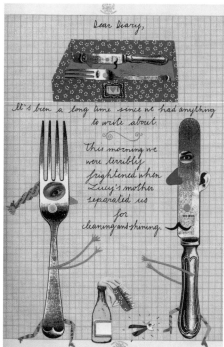

for that section is, not surprisingly, squared paper!'

She uses layout and composition cleverly in her treatment of the different parts. For example, here the chair spends most of its time alone, waiting for the children to come, then sitting in an empty school, so this spread has a bit of an empty feel to it, with the children's legs thundering in from the top, but lots of space elsewhere.

Expanding on the personalities of other main characters, Sara knows them so well she can sum them up perfectly. 'Bubu is very scruffy and makes mistakes, but you can tell from his style in general that he is an easygoing and likeable dog. His little quote says 'Dogs laugh, but they laugh with their tails'.

The girl, Lucy is bright and busy. She is the only human main character, and as Sara says, 'sort of represents the gay and curious spirit of childhood. That is also why she is drawn in a rather stylised way, she could have been a boy too! Her diary is the first one, so that the child reading the book can more easily identify with the story she/he is about to enter.'

Her introduction is the classic English poem by William Longfellow:

'There was a little girl
who had a litle curl
right in the middle of her forehead.
When she was good,
she was very, very good,
but when she was bad, she was horrid.'

The knife and fork think rather a lot of themselves and have very formal script handwriting to reflect that. They are isolated in their box, so to begin with they are frightened and a bit 'put out' to be taken out for the party. Spider writes in an inky, scratchy way. He is busy by nature, making clothes and rushing around. His diary introduces the events of the insects' world, taking us to a multicoloured and flamboyant masquerade insect party.

Whilst the project was a natural progression of Sara's existing working–style with its blend of the real and imaginary – its completion led her on to explore further in this 'autobiographical' vein. In the past few years, Sara Fanelli has gathered an impressive body of work, including many book jackets as well as illustrations for publications such as the *New Yorker*. She is modest about her achievements, but when pressed will give details.

'My handwriting has been used in several personal as well as commercial projects including a 40 meters timeline and 4 gallery walls at Tate Modern. But perhaps the longest-lasting influence *Dear Diary* had on me was a growing fascination with the wit and expressive conciseness that I came across whilst hunting for the little quotations that introduce each of the characters. In my research I found several inspirational texts, which led to a collection of illustrations. This body of work will be published in my next book, *Sometimes I think, Sometimes I am*, due to come out in Autumn 2007.'

She laughs and adds: 'It is just like the English saying 'One thing leads to another.' Funny to look back and see the links between a piece of work and another... A bit like the threads that connect bits of our life, as you can see when you read a diary!'

Dear Diary was published in hardback by Walker Books in 2000. A paperback version is now also available.

www.sarafanelli.com

PUSHING
AN
AROUND

Marc Valli talks to **Lee Williams** about how he turned his sketchbooks into the animation film *Tarot*

IDEA

I have known Lee Williams for some time. When I worked at the (now closed) bookshop Zwemmer, Lee was also a bookseller at the (now also closed) Dillon's Art bookshop on Long Acre. By the time my business partner and I were ready to start our own bookshop (Magma, still open), Lee had moved on and was working for art publisher Booth-Clibborn Editions. He then in turn helped set up the UK office of leading graphic-design publishers Die Gestalten Verlag, or dgv, as they are more widely known.

At Magma, Lee was always a familiar and popular figure. He would come down regularly to our Covent Garden shop to check how we were doing. He would slip in quietly and wander around checking the books until we had noticed him and then burst out laughing. Then you would certainly notice him. Lee has the loudest laugh in the town. But despite his regular visits and his spontaneous and garrulous nature, you could not help feeling that there was something unquestionably shifty about his behaviour. He had the inconspicuous ways of someone who's hiding something.

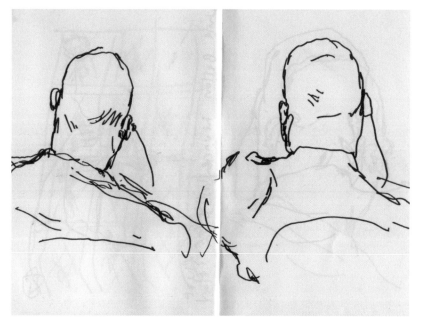

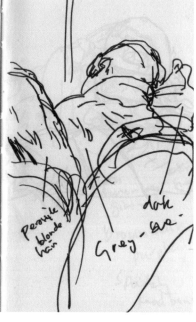

Above from top
A6 Sketchbook
A6 Sketchbook
A4 Sketchbook
Opposite and overleaf
Stills from 'Tarot' animation

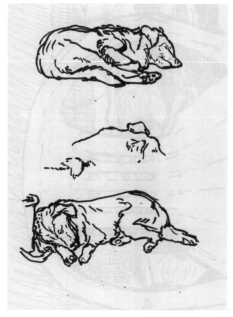

I knew he did not work full-time and I would wonder about what he did the rest of the time. When you asked him about it, he would become cagey and agitated. He would move even faster than he would normally do, flap the edges his raincoat, wipe his brow and hesitate, and this vagueness would continue to hover over the accounts of his activities outside work. Lee Williams seemed to be a man with a secret. As I would later find out (you can never hide anything for very long in the world of bookselling), Lee was leading a second life. Outside work, Lee Williams was also an artist.

Lee was trained in fine art at Bristol. He later did a postgraduate MA at the Royal Academy. At the Academy, Lee would sit three days a week for life drawing classes in this great room where Turner and Constable had trained. There were busts in the corridors. He found the place both imposing and inspiring.

But the world outside the Royal Academy's great room didn't have much in common with that of Turner and Constable. Britart was at its Zenith, with conceptual artists such as Damien Hirst and Sarah Lucas and Marc Quinn as its uncontested heroes. Tracey Emin had just put up her tent and Gavin Turk was dressing up dummies. All this, obviously, didn't have much to do with life drawing. And neither did the books Lee was dealing with on a daily basis. Lee would drift between parallel worlds. During the day, Lee inhabited the world of dgv and art produced on Apple Mac computers and websites and motion graphics and computer-generated characters. During his spare time, Lee explored the world of his own studio, a world devoid of flickering screens and buzzing G4s, a wilderness of pens and pencils and brushes and canvas and paper.

I only knew Lee as representative of the first world, the dgv one, until last year, when he told me about how he was finding a new creative freedom by revisiting that old skill: drawing. He had just been on holidays in Greece and he told me how, every afternoon, he would sit down with his sketchbook and draw anything that was around him, a dog that had been following him all day, his friend lying on the beach.

Upon his return from holidays, Lee started drawing London itself. He had always wanted to make something about London, about his love hate relationship with the city. He would catch glimpses of incidents from the bus and want to have them in picture form. He also wanted to document the atmosphere of London after the July bombs. Not making a big deal out of it, but just something that would express the tension in the background.

The next time I saw Lee, I asked him about his drawing and he surprised me by saying that it was evolving into something quite different. As he was working on his sketchbooks, he started noticing how drawings would show through the page. The fact that the drawings were showing through didn't bother him. On the contrary, the 'showing through' seemed to create something that was like movement. He thought it looked different and interesting and this is what gave him the idea of turning his sketchbooks into an animation film. He soon realised how closely related sketching and animation were. Not just in terms of technique and process, but also stylistically and even psychologically, how both reflected a certain impatience, as well as an obsession with movement and characters.

Lee tells me, as I am finally allowed into the sanctum of his studio, that he draws to find characters. They are very important to animation. He tells me he likes to capture people's small fidgety movements. Impatience. 'I am a real people watcher.' He tells me, 'I get told off quite often.'

Lee uses three different sizes of sketchbooks. He carries an A6 one with him all the time. He uses it to draw things like passengers on the bus, a balloon bouncing of a car, etc.

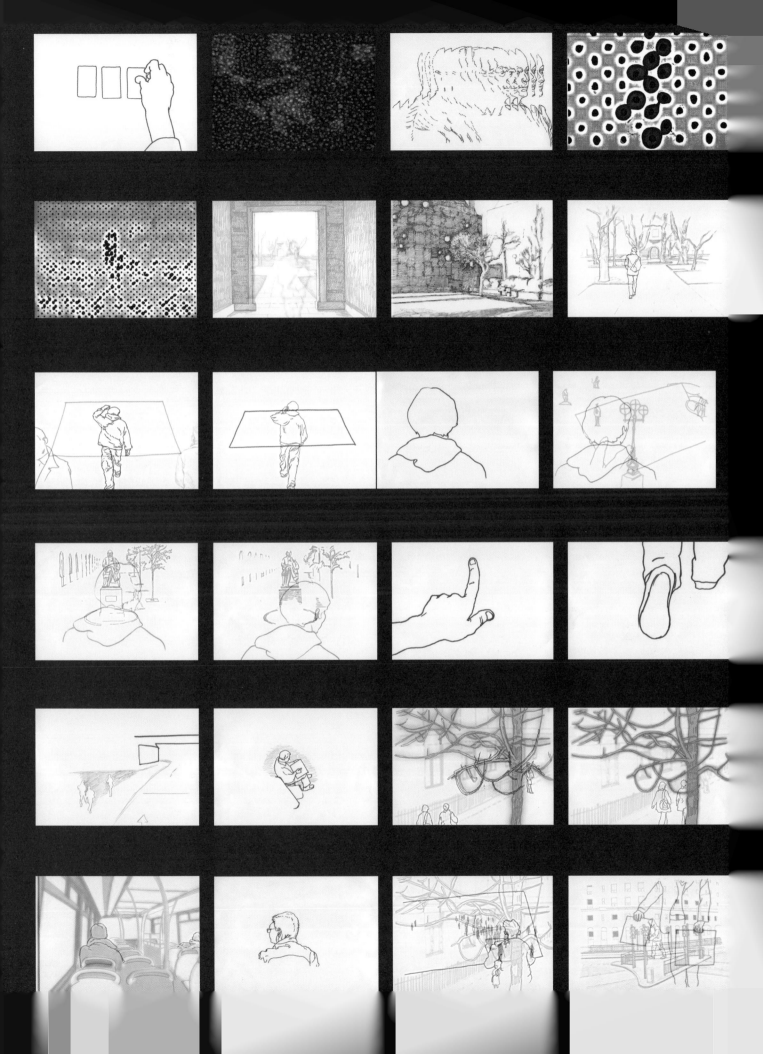

I ask him whether he finds drawing on a bus difficult? Yes, he agrees, and the result is often shaky. But he quite likes that. It makes the results more lively.

The format he uses most is the A5 sketchbook. He writes in them a lot, thoughts, things to look at, quotes. He points to one of them. It's by Paul Klee and says: 'taking a line for a walk,'

'I have always drawn.' Lee tells me as I leaf through the sketchbooks, 'For me drawing is a big deal. The academy was traditional, but the emphasis on drawing was very valid. Drawing is fundamental: it's investigating things. Quite a lot of contemporary painting uses found material, such as photographs, whereas drawing is a lot more personal. It's like pushing an idea around.'

'I use the sketchbooks to work on composition. They are more like the workbooks, really. There is a point where things become formulaic and working on the sketchbooks is a way of filtering that out. There may be one image in every two or three sketchbooks that I may want to investigate and take further.'

'I write lists in them too. I may pick up a word or two, then take it to the next notebook. Words are important. Words like 'slide', 'lantern', 'camera obscura', 'light from tv', 'flickering', 'infra-red', 'nightscape' – evocative words.'

Then the action moves onto an A4 format. This is where his animations start. Over the last two years Lee has filled 64 A4 sketchbooks and over 30 small ones. He numbers them. He keeps going back to them and making notes for reference.

I ask him about the title of his animation film. Why 'Tarot'?

'Tarot' he tells me, 'contains the idea of a spiritual journey, but also that of chance and that of images on cards and the act of laying those cards down. I like the connection to magic, the magic of making things move. And how animation itself started, as shadow play, after images, the Zoetrope.'

Obviously, the central character in the film is London itself. Lee tells me how in the mind of the observer the city builds itself, different elements appear and collide, becoming more frantic as you progress through the streets. Your eye has to flit around more.

'A lot of animation comes with a sense of narrative.' He adds, 'Mine doesn't. It's just images, layered.'

Even for someone as impatient as I am, *Tarot* lends itself very well to repeated viewing. Despite the absence of narrative, the flow of brilliantly hand-drawn images is both lively and hypnotic. I think of what Lee told earlier me about trying to capture the atmosphere of London after the July bombings and, yes, he did indeed manage to do that, capture the underlying tension between the rhythm of the city, of people going to work, and the sense that something big has happened, the sense that a big idea is being pushed around, shifted, silently, somewhere, somehow.

Now Lee is in the process of adding sound to the images. The sound of a projector, of voices, inside and outside. And, of course, music. Music, he tells me, smoothes things out. Makes you look at images in a different way.

With or without music, Lee Williams' film is very successful in recreating a sense of space and time and the interplay between the two. In this case the cliché is true: *Tarot* really is a journey. At the end of it, one feels very much like the main character, returning home at the end of the day, his mind filled images and dazed with a pleasant sensual saturation.

I also like to think that in his animation work Lee has managed to merge those two worlds: the ancient mystery of life drawing and a more modern, computer-generated brand of magic.

020-027:
RENATO ALÁRCAO

Renato Alarcão (born 1970) is a native of Rio de Janeiro. He studied graphic design at Rio's Federal University, followed by a Master's degree in illustration at NY School of Visual Arts and classes at the Center for Book Arts. His work has been published in magazines, newspapers, books, clients including *Playboy*, *The New York Times*, *Folha de São Paulo Newspaper*, Simon and Schuster, Penguin Putnam Books. He currently lives and teaches in Rio de Janeiro.

renatoalarcao@terra.com.br
www.renatoalarcao.com.br

Where does the personal stop and the professional begin? How much of your work is drawn from life?
There's no such line between personal and professional in my sketchbooks. Work is somewhat a stream of consciousness. I don't like to think much before I do something in my sketchbooks.

In terms of style, do you think 'personal' is a good thing?
Personal, or having personality, is paramount.

Do you use your work to exorcise elements from your life, or is work a hideout?
I used to work in my sketchbooks that way, therapeutically, catharsis on paper.

What's the most personal thing you'd be ready to share with us?
If it's too personal I prefer to keep it to myself. Especially my writing, which is more revealing than my imagery.

That was interesting, thank you. Now what about the truth?
Well, when I lost my brother, I kept my sanity thanks to my journal.

How important is the vernacular in your work?
It is as important as the images. But to me writing demands more energy, attention to some rules for clarity's sake. I believe I can be more intuitive and honest with my deepest feelings while working with visuals.

Do you take cameras and/or notebooks with you on holidays?
I find my travel snaps super boring, they never do justice to the things I see or experience. It's frustrating!

How good is your handwriting?
Very good. I always carry calligraphy pens with me.

Did you recall ever finding anything that completely changed your work or your outlook on something?
Not really. In my case I believe art is a process. One has to get involved in it, spend some time on it, build up experience one step at a time. I don't believe in people who claim they had a revelation that changed the way they see things. Maybe near-death experiences can cause that.

How would one go about creating map of your imagination?
Well, they should try starting with my sketchbooks. I am not so fond of my published commercial work.

Sometimes diaries make you want to weep and laugh. Sometimes they make you cringe. Sometimes it's all that at the same time. What about yours?
I've had people say they felt very emotional after reading my diaries, not woeful but a positive feeling.

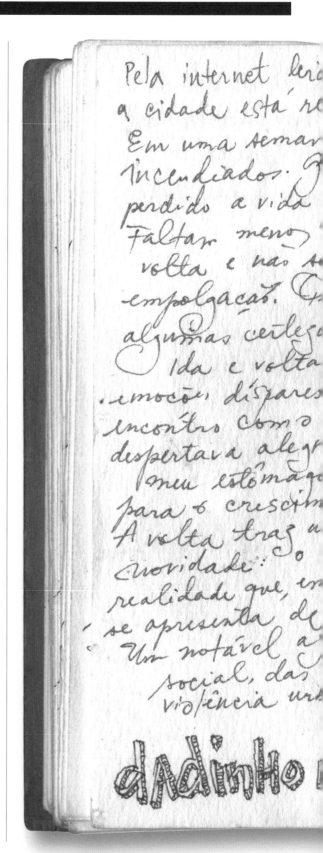

Title of work submitted:
Sketchbooks, graphic diaries, visual journals and photos
Date of completion:
From 2002 to 2006

Brief description of work submitted:
I call these books graphic journals or visual diaries. I collect whatever catches my attention, from found materials, drawings done on the spot, collages, graphic memorabilia, old stamps, calligraphy, text excerpts and interesting literary metaphors.

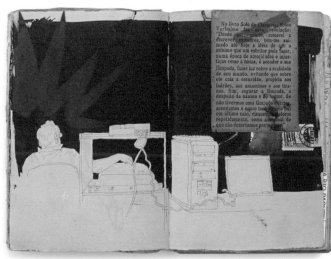

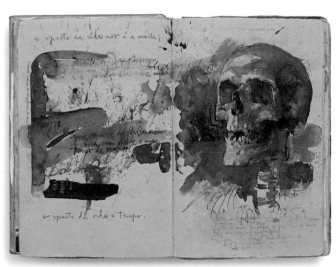

HOW TO DRAW

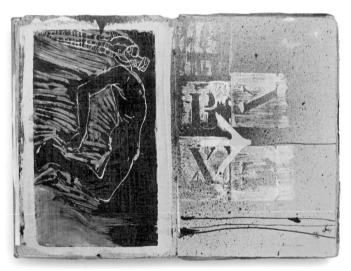

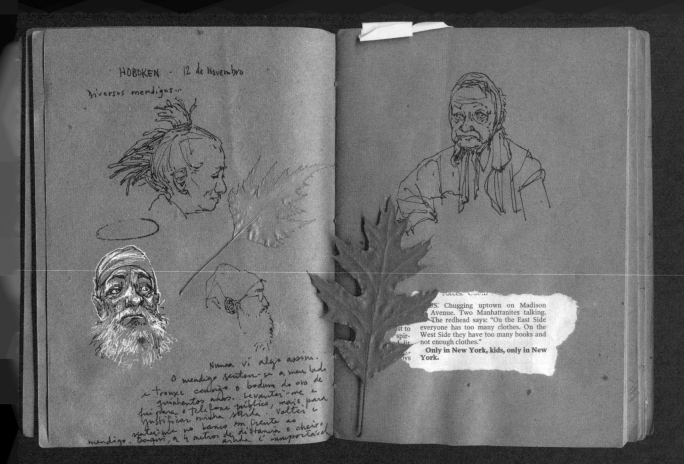

HOBOKEN - 12 de Novembro

diversos mendigos...

Nunca vi algo assim.
O mendigo sentou-se a meu lado
e trouxe consigo o bodum do ovo de
quinhentos anos. Levantei-me e
fui para o telefone público, mais para
justificar minha saída. Voltei e
sentei-me no banco em frente ao
mendigo. Porém, a 4 metros de distância o cheiro
ainda é insuportável

CIRCLE → perfection / completeness
freedom from distinction or separation
symbolizes the cosmic heaven (the
transcendent world of spirit in
particular its relation to earth
Concentric circles: Zen Buddhism
often employs drawings of concentric
circles to symbolize the
stages of inner perfection and the
progressive harmonization of the
spirit.
Sign of primordial unity. "All the
points on the circumference of a
circle are to be bound at its centre,
from which they originate and to which
they return.
It is also the symbol of time, the turning
wheel
In christian iconography the circle
symbolizes eternity.

Heaven (the circle) Earth (the square)
— mankind

God is a circle of which the centre
is everywhere

The fall of
Lucifer
(primarily the angel of the light
son of the dawn) Study 2

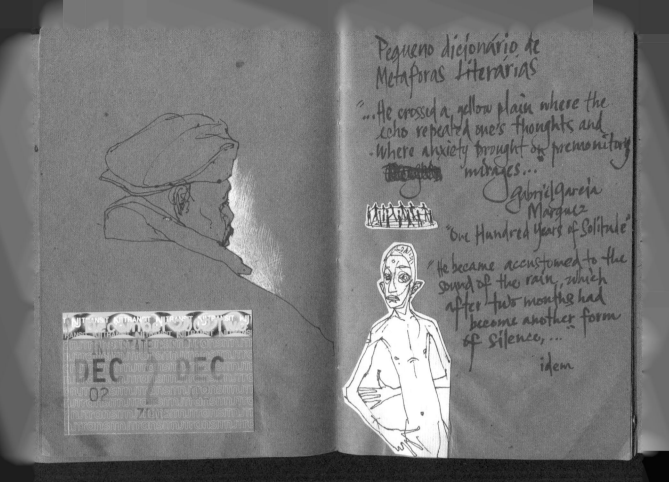

Pequeno dicionário de
Metáforas Literárias

"...He crossed a yellow plain where the
echo repeated one's thoughts and
where anxiety brought on premonitory
~~thoughts~~ mirages..."

Gabriel Garcia
Marquez
"One Hundred Years of Solitude"

"He became accustomed to the
sound of the rain, which
after two months had
become another form
of silence, ..."

idem

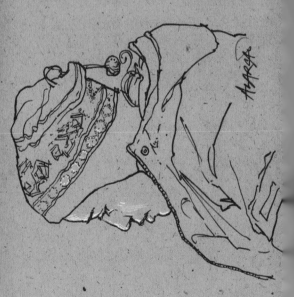

Commuters
Paterson. NJ
Winter 2003

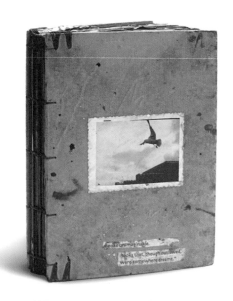

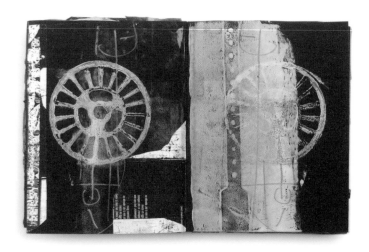

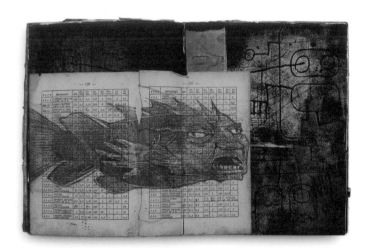

028-033:
REED ANDERSON

Reed was born in 1969. He grew up in a house surrounded by modern art, and spent a lot of time drawing and making forts. Now an artist and in search of a cheap and creative place to live, he recently drove across the country with his wife and son to California, where life feels oddly idyllic. He continues to work with cut paper drawings and relaxes by playing the banjo.

www.reedanderson.info

When do you look back? What do you do with your old diaries and notebooks?
I'll go through them if I am feeling uninspired. Of course this can go the other way too and make me feel like all is lost. I can usually squeeze something out of them though. They're like a well-loved sponge.

Do you use work to exorcise elements from your life, or is work a hideout?
In order to get to the grit of exorcising things, I think you need to hide out a little to trick the demons into thinking they are alone with you. Then trap 'em... afterwards you tame them, or conquer them by force. So it's a little bit of both.

Do you take cameras and/or notebooks with you on holidays? What's the result like?
I take a lot of pictures on holidays. I do super 8 as well. Something about watching super 8 is like seeing the reality of your memory unfold before your eyes; it is as you remember it. I've tried taking digital videos, but the appearance is too stark and too much like real life.

Do you scribble in the margins of books?
Yes, and it can be embarrassing later if you lend the book out. I lent a self-help book out without realising I had written all this stuff while I was trying to work some shit out. They called me and were like, man, you had a lot going on back then!

How would one go about creating a map of your imagination?
Have a gymnasium full of kids make a puppet show.

Sometimes diaries make you weep and laugh. Sometimes they make you cringe. Sometimes it's all that at the same time. What about yours?
Mostly I laughed at myself to see how profound I thought I was at whatever time I wrote something. Well, time changes everything...

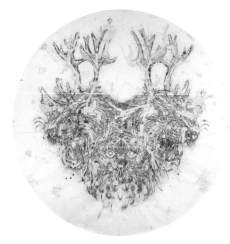

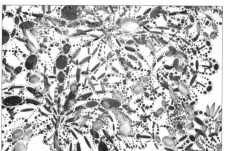

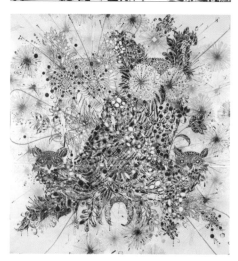

Above from top
'McCrackens Landing' (for Ned Skeed), 2006
8 feet round, Airbrush, acrylic, collage and silkscreen on cut paper
'The Kids Are Alright', 2006
65 inches x 54 inches, Pencil and liquid graphite on cut paper
'Where Are You Moriarty', 2005
7 1/2 feet x 7 feet, Airbrush, acrylic, collage and silkscreen on cut paper

Brief description of work submitted:
I once had someone read through my
notebooks and it took several years to get
over the feeling that someone was looking
over my shoulder. I try to be honest and
adhere to: 'First thought best thought'.

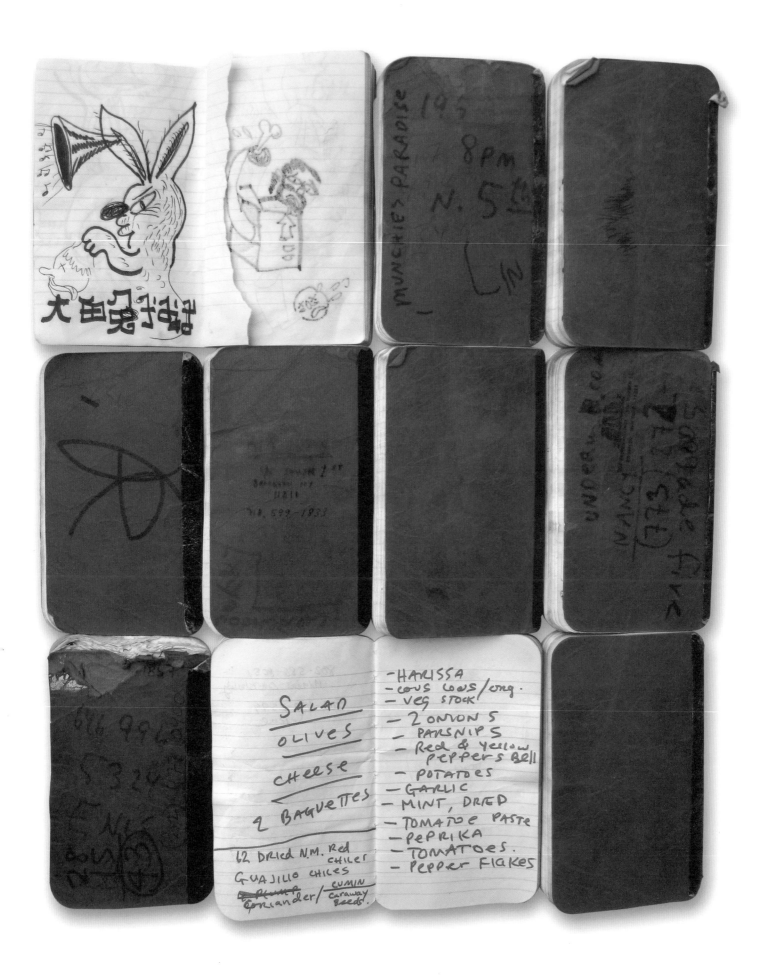

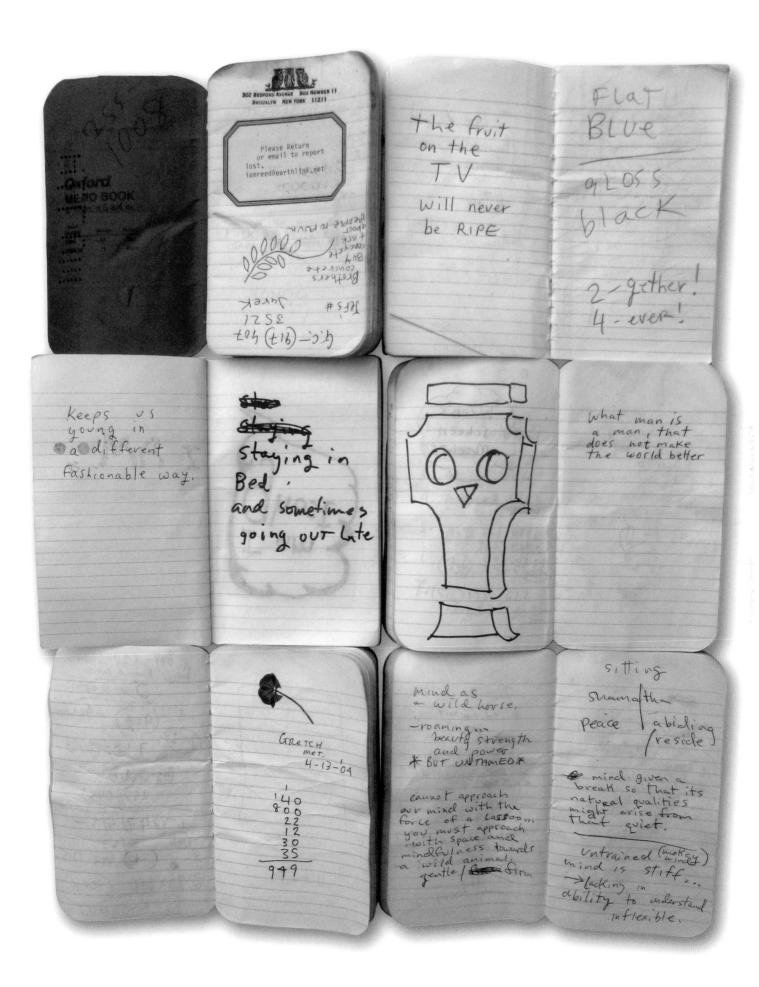

Oxford MEMO BOOK

302 BEDFORD AVENUE BOX NUMBER 11
BROOKLYN NEW YORK 11211

Please Return
or email to report
lost.
iamreed@earthlink.net

The fruit
on the
TV
will never
be RIPE

FLAT
BLUE

GLOSS
black

2-gether!
4-ever!

keeps us
young in
a different
fashionable way.

~~staying~~
staying in
Bed.
and sometimes
going out late

What man is
a man, that
does not make
the world better

GRETCH
met.
4-13-'04

140
800
22
12
30
35

949

mind as
a wild horse.
→roaming...
beauty strength
and power
* BUT UNTAMED *

cannot approach
our mind with the
force of a Lasso...
you must approach
with space and
mindfulness towards
a wild animal.
gentle/~~firm~~

sitting
shamatha
Peace / abiding
/ reside

mind given a
break so that its
natural qualities
might arise from
that quiet.

untrained (monkey)
mind is stiff...
→ lacking in
ability to understand
inflexible.

Hannah Barton is a young freelance illustrator based in London. While limited edition books and editorial work are her proffessional passions, cats, Orson Welles, comedy and playing the drums are her personal.

www.hannahbarton.com

Where does the personal stop and the professional begin? How much of your work is drawn from life?
I try to keep the appointments diary clear of jottings but I never manage it...there's notes and sketches throughout. In a way it seems pointless to separate the personal and professional too much as in my case they over lap a lot anyway.

What's the most personal thing you'd be ready to share with others (well, us)?
I have a bit of a crush on David Mitchell.

That was interesting, thank you. Now what about the truth?
I have a ganglion foot.

How important is the vernacular in your work?
Language and colloquialisms are really important to me. Words and phrases are a constant source of interest and I have an ongoing fascination with etymology. I love finding out how words and language developed.

Do you scribble on the margins of books?
No, though thinking about it, it's a good idea. I've just ever been inclined to.

How good is your handwriting?
My handwriting is terrible and at times illegible. I have to concentrate to write in even a remotely neat way.

Did you recall ever finding anything that completely changed your work or your outlook on something?
I've lost things, and perhaps the sensation of loss that has influenced me more than any one thing that I've found. You have more of an attachment to things that you're already familiar with so maybe that can create a bigger reaction. And the sensation of losing something that is irreplaceable is like nothing else.

Sometimes diaries make you want to weep and laugh. Sometimes they make you cringe. Sometimes it's all that at the same time. What about yours?
When I've looked back at diaries from when I was a little girl they bring back mixed emotions. I'm quite sentimental so I usually get a few nostalgia pangs. I find it hard to believe that a small version of me wrote those things, be they happy or sad. I think sentimentality comes from the sensation that a section of your life is over with, and you'll never go back to it. Reading diaries stirs up those feelings quite profoundly so they're usually a bittersweet moments in my experience, whatever the content of the entry.

Above From top

'Cup Happy'
(editorial piece, drawn with pens and pencils)

'Tape Collection'
(personal work, drawn with pens and pencils)

Title of work submitted: 'Supa Dupa' (pages 035-039) & examples of sketchbook pages (pages 040-041)
Date of completion: August 2006
Brief description of work submitted:
In 'Supa Dupa' I wanted to explore the way in which the creators of super-heroes give their characters incredible abilities but flaw them with human emotions and characteristics. The 'drawn' nature of characters always infers a personal touch, and never more so, than with super-heroes, where the creator has the ability to bestow the fantastic upon their creations. They are like fallible gods, providing justice in a secular society. They seem so modern to me. The increased popularity of comic book heroes is noticeably in sync with the decline of religious belief. They seem to fill a hole in our culture .

WOULD YOU BELIEVE THAT I AM FLAWED ONLY BY LOVE?

LOOK TO ME FOR GUIDANCE IF YOU WILL, BUT DON'T
FORGET THAT I AM FALLIBLE LIKE YOU. LEARN
NOT BY MIMICKING MY ACTIONS, BUT BY
RECOGNISING MY MISTAKES

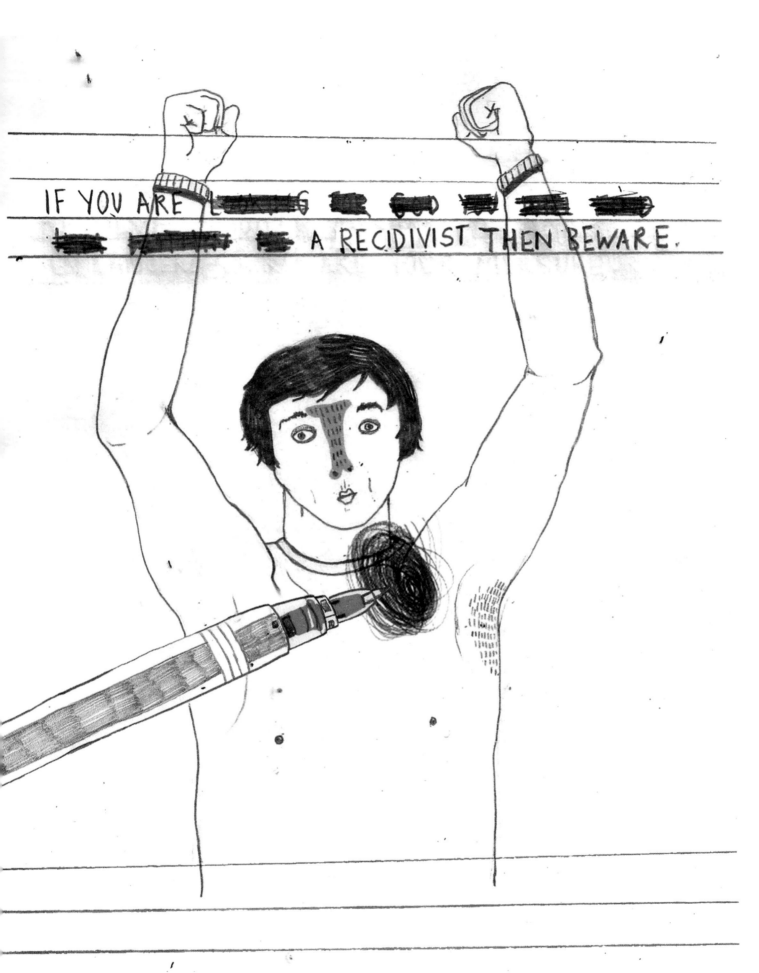

IF YOU ARE ~~LOOKING~~ ~~G~~ ~~███~~ ~~██~~ ~~███~~ ~~██~~ ~~████~~ ~~████~~ ~~███~~ ~~█████~~ ~~██~~ A RECIDIVIST THEN BEWARE.

I WILL PROTECT YOU AS BEST I CAN FROM ROBBERS,
THUGS, FIRES, LIONS, WINDS, RAINS, BAD GUYS,
EVIL-DOERS, ROCK STARS, GODS, DEVILS, YOUR
DEMONS, YOURSELF, YOUR COUNTRY, YOUR CULTURE.

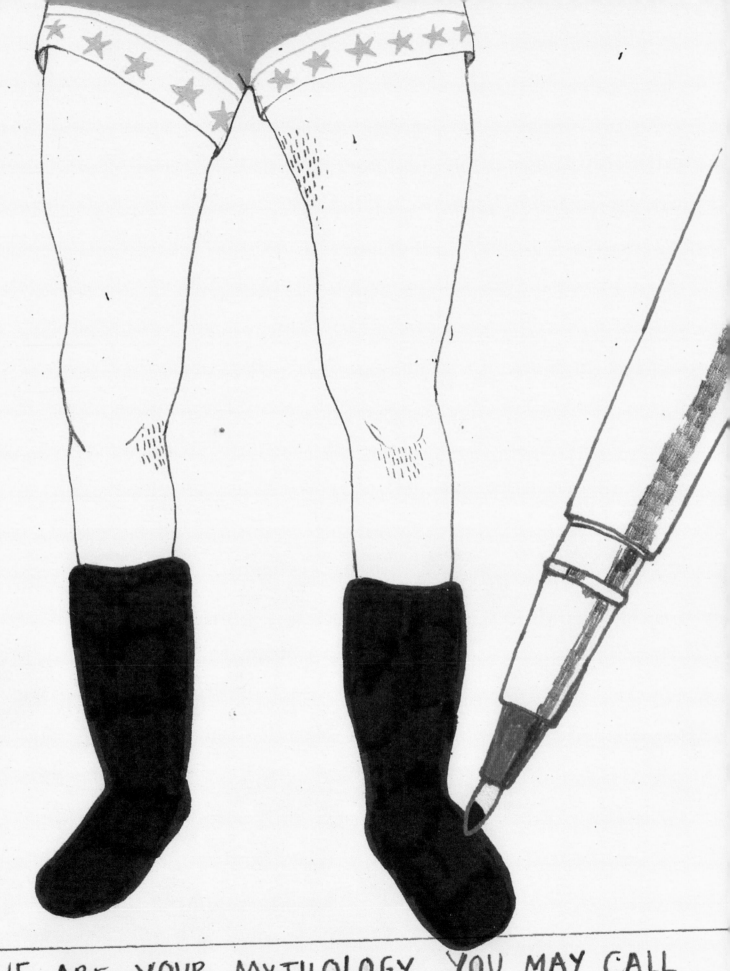

WE ARE YOUR MYTHOLOGY. YOU MAY CALL
ME ZEUS.

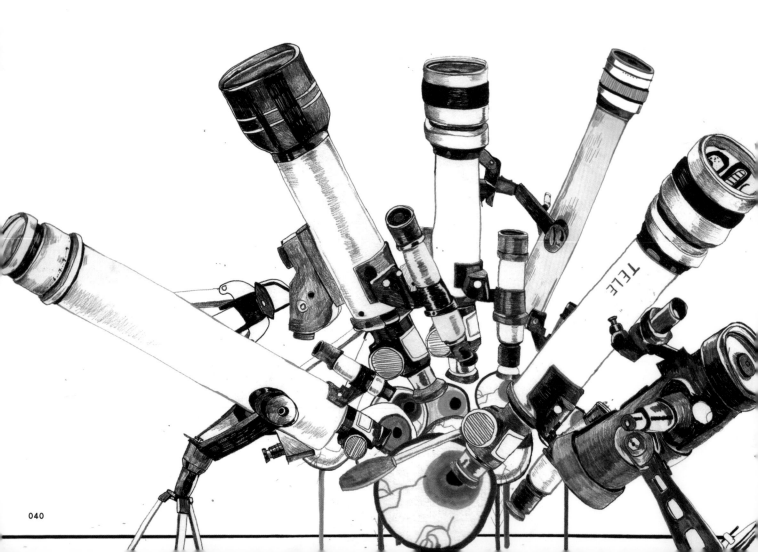

canovision 8

MY VIDEO

Base-V (Danilo Oliveira, Anderson Freitas, David Magila, Rafael Coutinho) is a group of artists from São Paulo, Brazil. In 2002 they started publishing the experimental magazine V. Afterwards, the magazine's website became an online community for experimental graphic art, exhibiting work from all over the world. The group works with all mediums: from arts publications to graphic installations, from gallery shows to street interventions. Base-V works to open space for free experimentation in graphical art and design.

www.base-v.org

Where does the personal stop and the professional begin? How much of your work is drawn from life?
In our personal productions the line is strongly defined. Each one of us has a unique way of working with images, which is a very positive thing for the group. Inside the group area, some works can be executed by a single person of the group, and that person will work in a very authorial way. Others are done by eight hands. The fact is that we are four individuals, with different perspectives on reality and life. Is TV life? I love TV. Are movies life?

In terms of style, do you think 'personal' is a good thing?
I believe any personal style comes from the perception and critique of other people's styles. But the search for it is far more important.

Do you use your work to exorcise elements from your life, or is work a hideout?
Any action to express an idea or a feeling exorcises something inside us. I believe the choice to work with visual skills, that choice itself, exorcises some stuffs and is a hideout for others.

Do you carry a bag with you? Could you list the items inside it?

Yesterday's newspaper, one jacket, a notebook, pencil and pens, some glue, some knives, grenades and chocolate cigars.

Do you take cameras and/or notebooks with you on holidays? What's the result like?
Yes, I think so. The result generally is: the notebook remains closed during the holidays, because holidays are very rare.

Do you work or think about work during your holidays?
Uh, yes. Sometimes. We are workaholics and almost alcoholics too.

What's your ideal holiday?
Nothing to do, distant from the city, beers, friends and good food.

Do you collect? What do you collect? Why?
Yes. Popcorn paper packages, VHS, graphic publications. Just because it's nice.

Did you recall ever finding anything that completely changed your work or your outlook on something?
Yes, sex has changed our lives.

Above from top
Other silkscreen poster
Illustration for 'Digitofagia' book
Detail from a silkscreen poster
Stencil poster

Title of work submitted: 'Collected Fragments'
Date of completion: 10 July 2006
Brief Description of work submitted:
This new series from Base-V is produced by
eight hands. All the actual members from
the group are involved. We think any creative
process passes by a juncture of fragments,
of experiences, references, ideologies.

This series tries to use our day-by-day
production and brainstorming, graphically
represented, in order to create other spheres
of communication.

During production, individual skills
lose their importance, creating a more open
concept, a free boarding on the authoral
issues. The drawings, initially produced as

sketches of ideas and individual experiences,
are now united in a one-peace-work, and
acquires a collective identity.

We tried to keep the drawings as they were,
raw and expressive, usually drawn on white
paper, using only few spaces for colors.

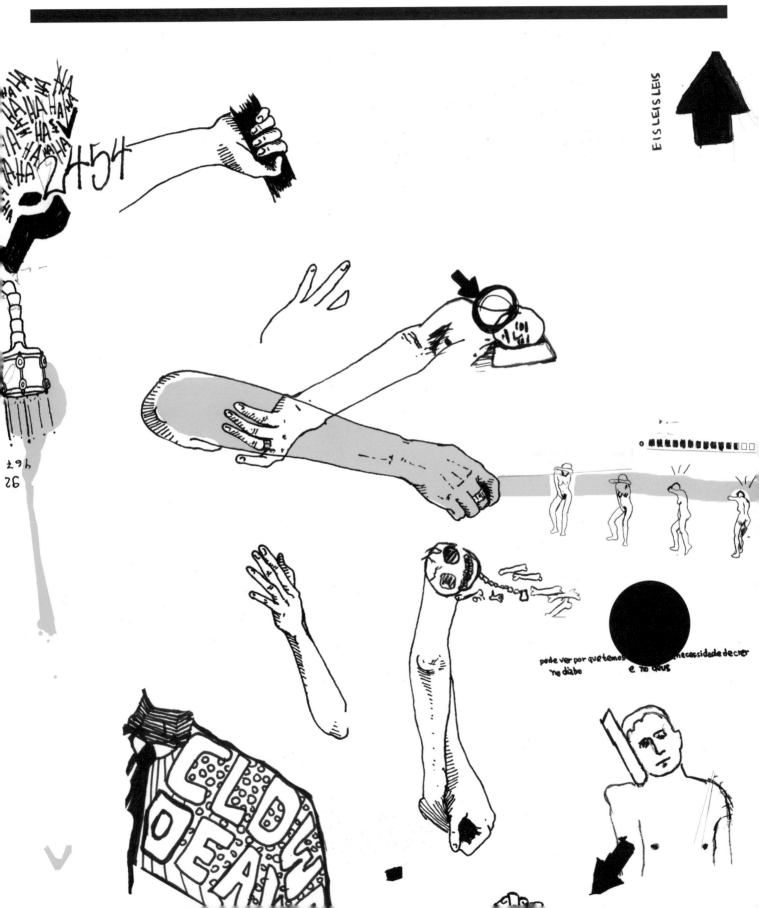

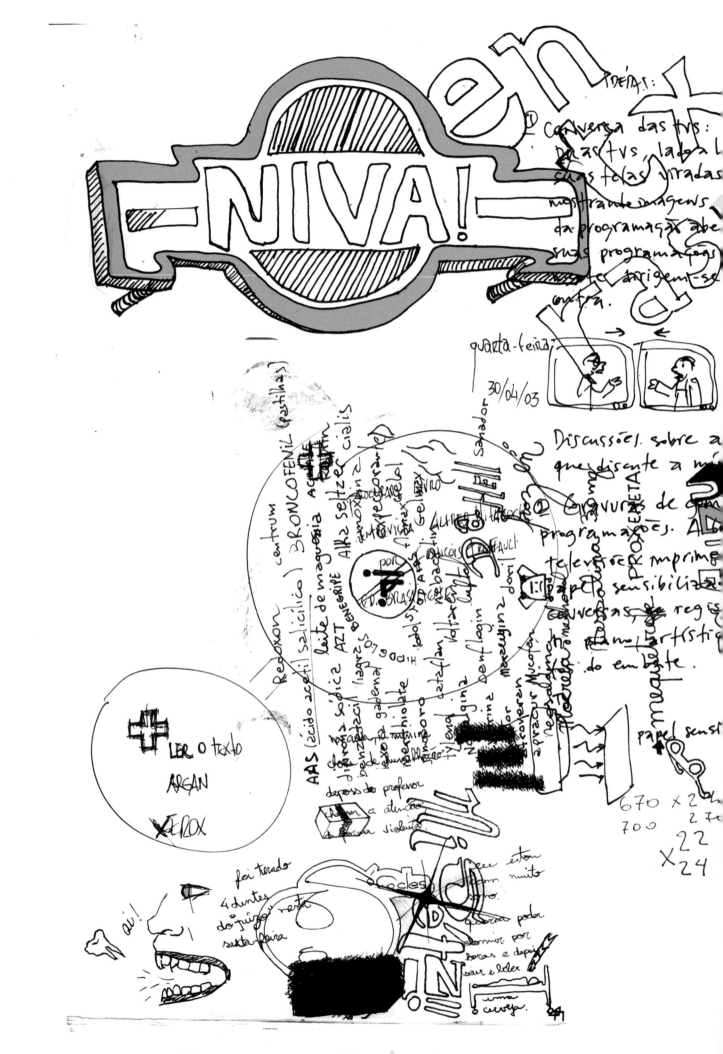

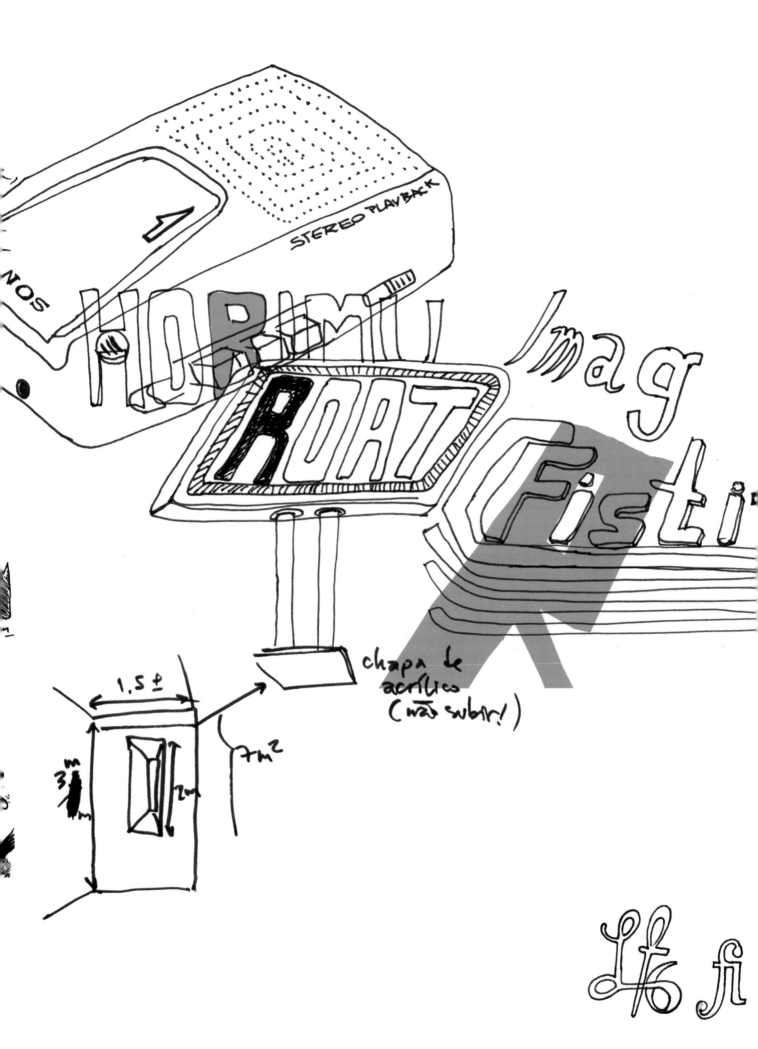

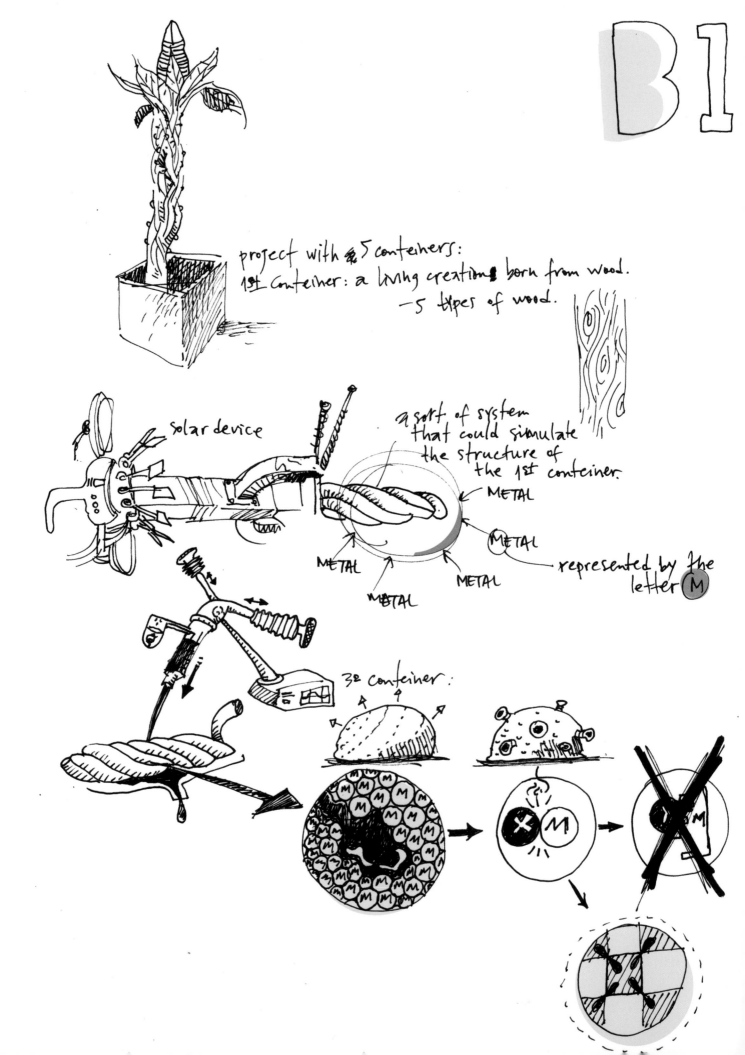

B1

project with 5 conteiners:
1st Conteiner: a living creatione born from wood.
— 5 types of wood.

solar device

a sort of system that could simulate the structure of the 1st conteiner.

METAL

METAL

METAL

METAL

METAL

represented by the letter M

3º conteiner:

4th container: ships coming from the sea.

fishes created from cruising with other genotypes, such as flowers and potatoes, under soil.

C2

obs: the 5th container is filled with heavy emotions; between 500 kg and 2 tons. Not defined yet.

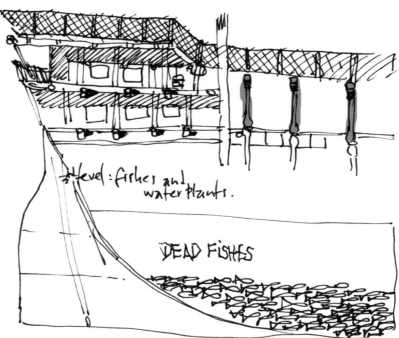

4th level: fishes and water plants.

DEAD FISHES

EXTINGUISHED

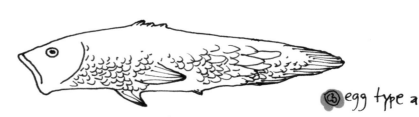

Pincilatitutu Nemensis

⊛ egg type a

cowini piscinrifalsi

🦴 type b

invect nest

Midisaizinvest

✳ no eggs

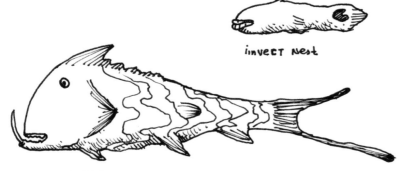

Natufipiscin shiaisn

050-055:
JON BURGERMAN

Jon Burgerman is an artist and illustrator based in Nottingham. His work, often consisting of mangled characters and colourful environments has appeared in many books, magazines, websites and galleries around the world.

www.jonburgerman.com

Are you honest with yourself on your diary?
Nope, it's all one big lie.

When do you look back? What do you do with your old diaries and notebooks (apart from submitting them to graphic)?
They are kept in a cupboard, stacked up high, taking up valuable room. Sometimes I'll flick through old ones and lament all my wasted time.

Where does the personal stop and the professional begin? How much of your work is drawn from life?
It's a blurred line which I used to think was a good thing but now realise probably isn't.

Do you use your work to exorcise elements from your life, or is work a hideout?
Work is a giant monster that consumes everything. You're stuck in the belly of the beast wondering where you are, what that swimming noise is and who else is down here.

What's the most personal thing you'd be ready to share with others (well, us)?
I don't actually think I have anything I could share. There's nothing I can think of right now. I'd be happy to share my date of birth if that meant you'd buy me a present.

That was interesting, thank you. Now what about the truth?
I steal mushrooms off the floor at the local market when no one's looking.

Do you stop in the middle of the street to make a note in your diary or take a picture? What kind of notes? What kind of pictures?
Not really, not unless I really really have to write something down. Generally I'll try and keep things in my brain and hope my phone doesn't ring or I bump into anyone I know on the way home.

Do you take cameras and/or notebooks with you on holidays? What's the result like?
Yes. The result is always underwhelming.

Do you write postcards?
I used to but no-one ever sends me postcards anymore so I'm cutting back on the amount I send. My parents went on holiday and my dad got me a postcard but he post it. When I saw them after they got back he gave it to me. It was blank on back.

Did you recall ever finding anything that completely changed your work or your outlook on something?
Seeing Jean-Michel Basquiats work for the first time when I was little had a big affect on me. Nothing that major since but I do come across lots of great things that inspire me and add to my feeling of worthlessness in equal measure.

How bad is your telephone bill?
It's from Bulldog, who are not very good at accurately calculating it (they've yet to send a bill without a mistake on it), so it's very bad indeed.

How would one go about creating map of your imagination?
Get a bag of crisps, stamp on it, sprinkle over cake crumbs, add pencil sharpenings, soil, tofu chunks and spaghetti and then wait for a bit. Clean up the mess, put the kettle on and stop being so silly.

Sometimes diaries make you want to weep and laugh. Sometimes they make you cringe. Sometimes it's all that at the same time. What about yours?
It's all that at the same time, I don't know. It's better to look forward though, isn't it? Better to be positive. Anyway, you shouldn't believe everything you read, even if you're the one who's written it.

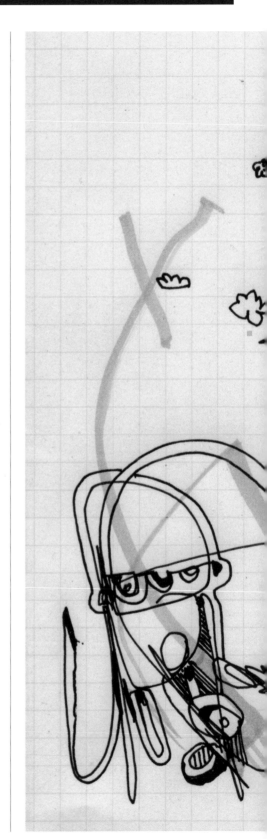

Brief description of work submitted:
'Biro-web Diary' was commissioned by
the BBC after they'd visited my website
www.biro-web.com. It features my exaggerated
real-life neurotic thoughts set out as diary
entries. The other collection of pieces, 'Handy
Jotter', is in a similar but more skewed vein.
Date of completion: 2004

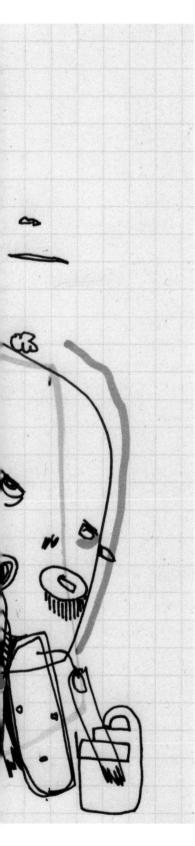

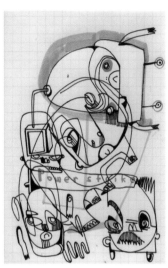

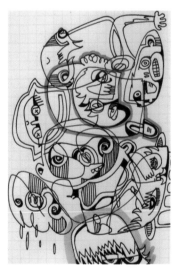

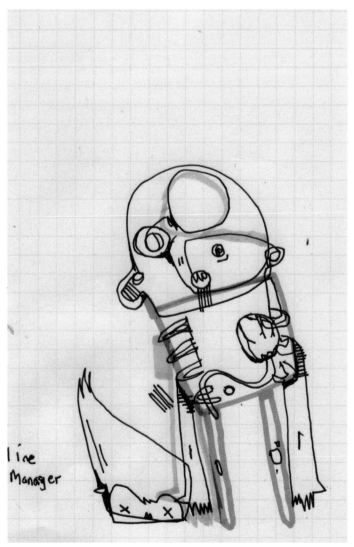

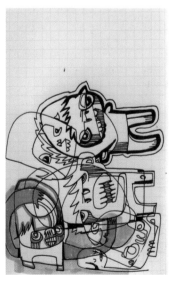

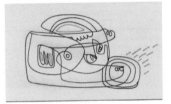

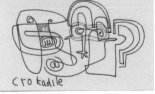

8 Monday
313–53

9 Tuesday
314–52

10 Wednesday

Starburst fruit chew, found on street corner.
[unopened]

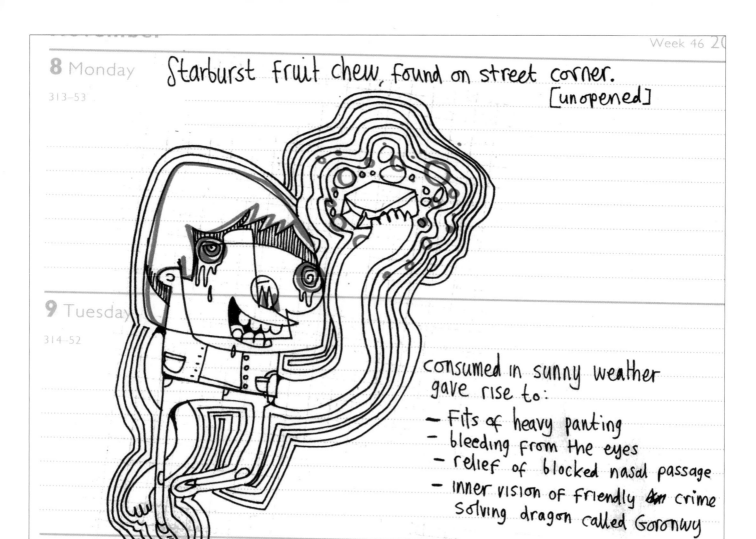

consumed in sunny weather
gave rise to:

- Fits of heavy panting
- bleeding from the eyes
- relief of blocked nasal passage
- inner vision of friendly crime solving dragon called Goronwy

---

Constant thudding

Friday 26

and soft mutterings at 3am

→ Next door neighbours are young student types, with their outlandish hair + large trousers

Saturday 27

RAD KID

WIL KID

RAD DUDE!

Let's drink and party

and then set off a smoke alarm

Strange smells seep from their windows — invading precious clean air space.

Sunday 28

egg fish bad

Retreat

→ under dining room table - listen but try not to listen...
...Can clearly hear laughter + fun through the walls. must phone police

November

PLEDGE

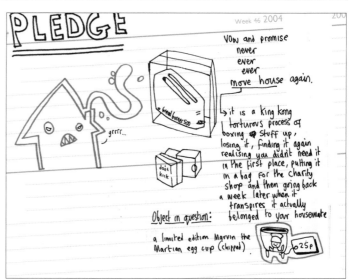

grrrr...

bread bin er 500

dont kick

Vow and promise
never
ever
ever
move house again.

→ it is a king kong torturous process of boxing @ stuff up, losing it, finding it again realising you didn't need it in the first place, putting it in a bag for the charity shop and then going back a week later when it transpires it actually belonged to your housemate

Object in question:
a limited edition Marvin the Martian egg cup (chipped)

25p

There IS Life on mars

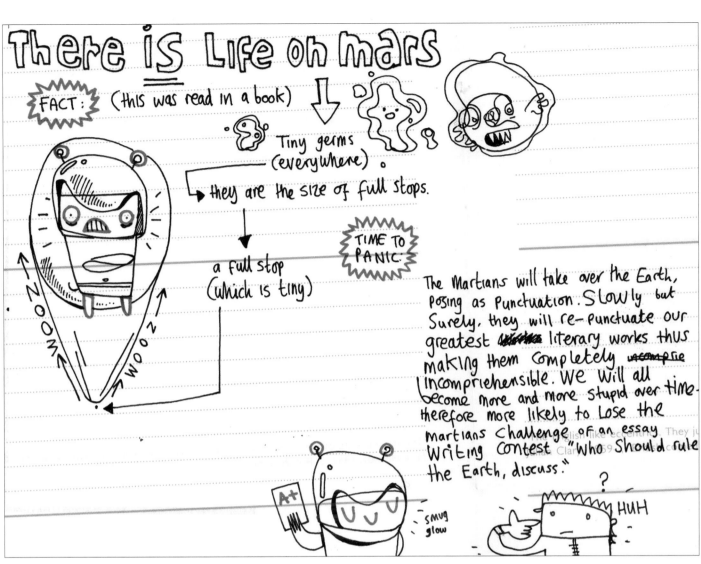

FACT: (this was read in a book)

Tiny germs (everywhere)

they are the size of full stops.

a full stop (which is tiny)

TIME TO PANIC:

ZOOOM
WOOZ

The Martians will take over the Earth, posing as punctuation. Slowly but surely, they will re-punctuate our greatest ~~works~~ literary works thus making them completely ~~incompre~~ incomprehensible. We will all become more and more stupid over time. therefore more likely to lose the Martians challenge of an essay writing contest "Who should rule the Earth, discuss."

A+

smug glow

? HUH

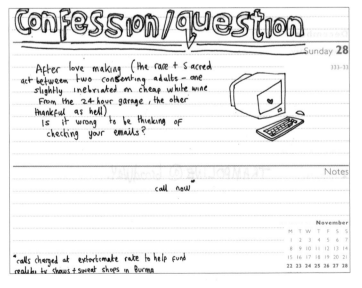

confession/question

After love making (the rare + sacred act between two consenting adults — one slightly inebriated on cheap white wine from the 24 hour garage, the other thankful as hell)
is it wrong to be thinking of checking your emails?

Notes

call now*

November
M T W T F S S
 1 2 3 4 5 6 7
8 9 10 11 12 13 14
15 16 17 18 19 20 21
22 23 24 25 26 27 28

*calls charged at extortionate rate to help fund reality tv shows + sweat shops in Burma

---

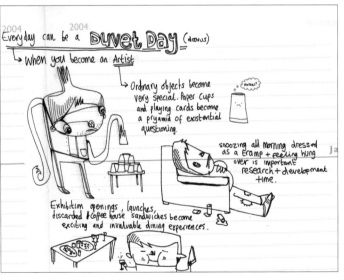

2004   2004

Everyday can be a **Duvet Day** (dcovus)

→ When you become an Artist

→ Ordinary objects become very special. Paper cups and playing cards become a pyramid of existential questioning.

snoozing all morning dressed as a tramp + feeling hung over is important research + development time.

Exhibition openings, launches, discarded ~~k~~ coffee house sandwiches become exciting and invaluable dining experiences.

056–059:
DANIEL DAVIDSON

Born 1965 in San Francisco. Lives and works in Brooklyn, NY. His work is a fusion of hybrid characters, spaces and styles. Often employing the comic and the grotesque, he examines the multiple and fractured personalities of a cobbled identity. He has had a series of exhibitions throughout the US.

In terms of style, do you think 'personal' is a good thing?

For me it is – I think I tried to dance around it. But remember, it's hard to look cool when you're making a painting about how fat you feel.

Do you stop in the middle of the street to make a note in your diary or take a picture? What kind of notes? What kind of pictures?

I am the type who does that. I also pick up a lot of trash I see on the street. I'm making an armada of spaceships out of plastic pieces that I find and hot-glue together. Bottle caps, lids, cool trash. I'm afraid it's become an obsession.

How good is your handwriting?

Good enough, better than my doctor, not as good as my mom who learned the 'Palmer Method' of writing in her school.

Do you collect? What do you collect? Why?

People who collect stuff are weird in a way. I had collections as a kid. I collected as many different types of beer bottle caps as I could find, keeping them in a band-aid tin. I would smell the bottle caps for the smell of beer which subconsciously reminded me of my dad who died when I was two. My brother collects guns, furs, nunchucks and knives, then photographs them and calls it his 'arsenal'.

Sometimes diaries make you want to weep and laugh. Sometimes they make you cringe. Sometimes it's all that at the same time. What about yours?

The capacity to fail is inherent in the best artmaking – if someone gives you a piece of paper and says 'make me a great drawing' you're more likely to fail, but if they give you a hundred sheets, sooner or later you will try the stupid thing that's actually the brilliant thing to do.

Above from top
'Mirror Cop' 2006
19" x 30" watercolour on paper
'Mirror Miner' 2006
19" x 30" watercolour on paper
'Mirror Miner Skull' 2006
11" x 14" watercolour on paper

Brief description of work submitted:
My wife says you shouldn't write down
something unless you're comfortable with
everyone reading it. The tobacco execs and
Martha Stewart's stockbroker can certainly
attest to that. I am honest, because otherwise,
what's the point? Wishful thinking – at best.
Waste of time to lie to your shrink.

060-063:
DAISY DE VILLENEUVE

Daisy de Villeneuve was born in London in 1975. She studied Fashion & Fine Art in New York and Paris. Daisy has written and illustrated two books which draw upon her life experiences, *He Said She Said* and *I Told You So*, and featuring her trademark style of felt tip pen and typewriter text. De Villeneuve has collaborated with Topshop, Heal's and the Victoria & Albert Museum. She regularly contributes to magazines such as *Elle Girl Korea*, *Cheap Date*, *Nylon* and *British Vogue* as both a writer and illustrator. In 2004 she had her first major solo show at the Fashion & Textile Museum in London.

daisy@daisydevilleneuve.com
www.daisydevilleneuve.com

Are you honest with yourself on your diary?
Yes. Sometimes I'll leave out the really personal things. Or I write X for a person or a thing & then a couple years later I'll look back & think, 'who the fuck was X?'.
What do you have in your pockets when you leave the house?
Tissues, gum, loose change, maybe a lipstick & my oyster card.
Do you carry a bag with you?
Yes.
Could you list the items inside it?
Wallet, keys, make-up bag, notebook, day journal, A-Z, pen, glasses, iPod, mobile, umbrella & camera.
Do you collect?
Yes. What do you collect? I collect tins. I get these huge old potato chip & lard tins from Michigan, USA, that I store all my pens in. I also collect Royal memorabilia (but I try not to overdo it, because it could get really OTT).
How would one go about creating map of your imagination?
Get a massive piece of paper, some pens & start scribbling.

'the best way to get over a man is to get under another' she said.

Above from top
Postcard for Topshop
'Tyler' courtesy of Fashion Art

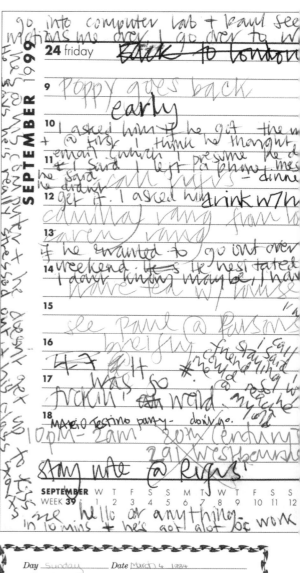

Title of work submitted: Daisy's dairies
Date of completion: 30 August 2006
Brief description of work submitted:
The work that I have submitted are all old pages from my diaries & notebooks over the years, ranging from 1984-2005. My diaries, notebooks and all the little trinkets/ephemera I keep are always a great source of inspiration.

Plus they have sentimental value to me in their own way. I have included some personal pieces too that I have collected over the years. Some of those things include: a postcard given to me by a stranger on the subway in New York ten years ago, my answering machine messages on my 16th birthday, a country club card from Indiana in 1991 and a polaroid of me aged 11.

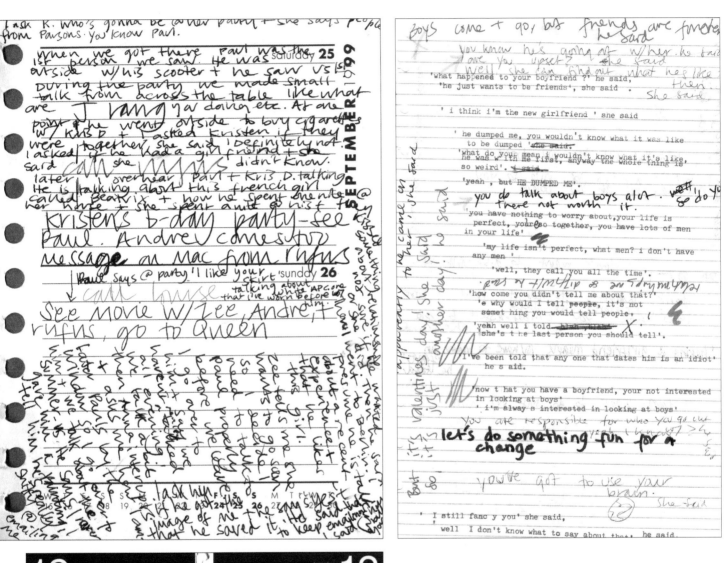

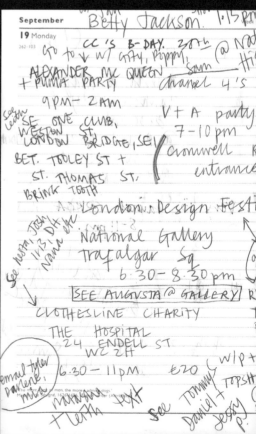

BETSY'S ANSEK-
ING MESSAGES
ON HER 16TH
JUNE 5TH 1991

AUGUST 1998

7 friday

09.00

10.00

Breakfast out w/ Tal

11.00

12.00 He said "I's Alexy don't go see that movie w/
cameron diaz because I want you to see it
w/ me it you come to L.A. I said
why cant you go see it w/ someone else He said cos everyone's seen it
13.00 said guess how much it costs to get to
$1000 the cheapest ticket is $600 he
said thats not bad I said I could afford
it Then we talked for a little bit
14.00 more then he was like - yeah bye"

15.00 Alex rang

Charles rang cool Joes

P + J rang

16.00

17.00

18.00

evening   go out for drink
w/ Joe

AUGUST S S M T W T **F** S **S** M T W T F
WEEK 32 1 2 3 4 5 6 **7** 8 **9** 10 11 12 13 14

NOTE: CALL   **March—April 1994**
CHARLES   **Thursday 31**
                  Maundy Thursday
go to Dentist
• start Antibiotics
  Amoxicillian
  Nanny arrives
    in Indy
I am so nervous/worried about
going back to New York, stupid
#FUCK them PRICKS
                  Friday 1
                  Good Friday
                  Holiday UK
I had a right to be
felt crap when I went
April Fools Day   back
Lunch at Kitchen
call Darlene (place)
go watch movie 'The House
                  of Spirits'
Andy to N.Y. w/ Poppy
                  Saturday 2
lunch at + dinner out
go to Basketball Game
  Indiana vs Orlando (Shaquille)
Pacers   Magic with O'Neil
                  Sunday 3
                  Easter Day
                  easter
                  . day

Bartender: SARA
"WHAT DO U NORMALLY DRINK?" He's asked to get
u more drinks, "GET HER ANOTHER
drink."
Said something about losing by we kissed.
Kissed @ Tottenham court Rd tube station.
I HAVE YOUR NUMBER? He won't
put it in phone, came behind me 2 hold
on 2 me.

HELD OUT ARM 2 HOLD
IN CAR He put his hands over 2
warm them up.

"YOUR MAKE UP SMELLS BEAUTIFUL"
  or ... PERFUME

IN MIDST CONVERSATION -
SOMETHING I LOVE U.

WANTS 2 TAKE ME OUT WHEN WE R BOTH
SOBER.

Guest Membership

RIVIERA CLUB

Name   Daisy de Villeneuve   16

Address   10218 Indian Lake

Guest of   Betsy Griswold

Void After   AUG 28 1991

This guest card is required for admission   382

FEBRUARY 1990

12 MONDAY

13 TUESDAY
Joe over

Emma phones

14 WEDNESDAY   SPEAK TO
Valentines Day   Betsy

SUCKS SO MUCH!!!

15 THURSDAY

September   Betty Jackson 1:15 pm
19 Monday   CC's B-DAY 30th
262-103   go to w/ Gitty, Poppy,
ALEXANDER MC QUEEN
+ PUMA PARTY   channel 4's
9pm-2am   V + A party
SEE ONE CLUB,   7-10 pm
WESTON ST.   (Cromwell R
LONDON BRIDGE, SE1   entrance
BET. TOOLEY ST +
ST. THOMAS ST.
BRINK TOOTH
                London Design Festi
                National Gallery
                Trafalgar Sq
                6.30-8.30pm
                [SEE AUGUSTA @ GALLERY]
CLOTHESLINE CHARITY
THE HOSPITAL
24 ENDELL ST
WC2H
email tyler 6.30-11pm   £20
Darlene!

MELANIES B-DAY

Beverly Wilshire Hotel

Dear Poppy & Daisy

I thought you both
would like a letter from
HOLLYWOOD. I look forward
to seeing you on my return.
much love & kisses.

Daddy

P.S. I've told Mickey Mouse
(who lives here) about you two!
P.S.S. AND Donald Duck!

H. FROM

SEE TEO

GO FOR
DRINK W/
HIM @
GRAND UNION.

ED OVERNITE

AUGUST 1998

7 friday

09.00

10.00

11.00 Breakfast out w/Tal

He said "If Alex don't go see that movie w/
Cameron Diaz because I want you to see it
w/ me. if you come to L.A. I said
why can't you go see it w/ someone else he said m/g everyone's seen it
I said guess how much it costs to get in
I said $1000, the cheapest ticket is $900
said that's not bad I said I don't a damn
it. then we talked for a little bit
about then he was like - yeah bye.

12.00

13.00

14.00

15.00 Alex rang
Charles rang Cari Joes
P + J rang

16.00

17.00

18.00

evening Go out for drink
w/ Tal

AUGUST WEEK 32   S S M T W T **F S S** M T W T F
1 2 3 4 5 6 **7 8 9** 10 11 12 13 14

H. R. Giger

Not to bother you or anything but would
you be interested in doing something sometime?
My name is Blue and unfortunately I'm on
my way to work. I want to make

blue
674-3892

No Tal

---

2 MOXON ST   September
Tuesday **20**

CAMILLAS B-DAY.

12·15 pm meet Dakiah
for lunch @ FROMA

BURBERRY'S PARTY
4 MICHEAL ROBERTS

Serge
4:30 pm

BOOK LAUNCH
21 - 23 NEW BOND S
W/

MFORD'S PARTY
6·30 - 9 pm

NPG COMITTEE MEETING
6-8 pm @

MICY
ANNIE,
LEITH etc
W/ Jan   Hannah B

ElIE DECORATION
DESIGN AWARDS
@ LIBERTY

7:30 PM DOORS OPEN
8:30 PM PRESENTATION on 4th FL
10:30 PM END

September
5 6 7 8 9 10 11
12 13 14 15 16 17 18
19 20 21 22 23 24 25
26 27 28 29 30

Adrian W. left message

December 2002   Week 49

$748.40 $55-$40

American Airlines

2 Monday (336-29)   Depart London Heathrow
12·15 pm

arrive 3 pm JFK
go to gallery   I love
them
$595.00

go to lovely day for dinner
go to Bliss bar

3 Tuesday (337-28)   Augusta's 21st B-day
Poppy + Sali arriving 4pm

1·30 NEWARK
Annie rang   message from Tal
call Tal in London

dinner @ pink pony w/ Mom

4 Wednesday (338-27)   Natasha + Molly Monday
Jane arrives

lunch @ Mickey Day
w/ Sali, Poppy + Annie

December 2002   Week 49

$286.4
212. $61.76

Thursday 5 (339-26)   Ivan: photo shoot
American Vogue

Molly arrives   email
dev
Sali
lunch w/ Joe
CALL VALERIE IN LONDON
dinner w/ Simon + his friends @ Rivals

Friday 6 (340-25)   OPENING OF SHOW
Zac
Alas, Lorenzo, Joe, Piers, Seth, about 7pm
Andrew Ege. After party   Simon came
go to Pana bar + John St @ 10-12
K rang from U.K.

Saturday 7 (341-24)   call Joe, see
text Seth go to see Zac Tara
brunch w/ Miranda Molly, Ivan, Mum
Greg Morris party

Leave N.Y.

Sunday 8 (342-23)   Kig → Cleve
La Guardia 10·30 am
Dinner w/ Uncle Jim etc @ Country Club

1996 December   [Week 51]

16 Monday   Leave Florida
Breakfast at Waffle House w/
Kerri + Kevin

17 Tuesday

18 Wednesday

19 Thursday   go to Nan Golden show
w/ Zee

20 Friday   Leave NYC

21 Saturday   Back home

Vde V for breakfast w/ Perry's
22 Sunday   See Tim in Hawksley -
Inn go w/ Tessa, Poppy,
Ramana + Zara
Tessa stays night.

064-073:
HENRIK DELEHAG

Henrik Delehag is one half of Benrik. Founded with Ben Carey in 2003, Benrik's mission is to spread a little anarchy in people's lives. *This Diary Will Change Your Life*, now in its fourth year, gives its disciples a life-changing task every day, ranging from 'Today do a runner' to 'Today propose to a complete stranger'. So far they have sold over 350,000 copies worldwide.

www.benrik.co.uk
www.thiswebsitewillchangeyourlife.com

Do you scribble into notebooks?
I don't like to keep scribbles. If my notebook is messy, my life is a mess, and vice versa. I spend several hours with my book a day, so it's a relationship. Many ideas become better if you treat them well. And knowing they will be treated well, they keep on coming.
Are you honest with yourself on your diary?
This is the constant battle. Honesty only goes as far as you can stretch it. Sometimes I'm honest, sometimes I pretend to be.
Where does the personal stop and the professional begin?
To me, if it's not personal it's not professional.
In terms of style, do you think 'personal' is a good thing?
It depends on the person.
What's the most personal thing you'd be ready to share with others (well, us)?
My middle name is Kenneth.
That was interesting, thank you. Now what about the truth?
The truth is that they are coming to get us. Me and Ben have seen traces. There are branches missing in the trees. They've been collecting.
Do you collect? What do you collect? Why?
I don't collect. Collections make your life bigger on the outside when you should be making your life bigger on the inside.
How would one go about creating map of your imagination?
Benrik are currently in the process of mapping out our mutual brain. The result will be published in 2009.

Title of work submitted:
Sketchbook
Date of completion:
2003-2006
Brief description of work submitted:
I keep a notebook diary. It's a very thick tome
with a hard cover. It takes me about two years
to fill one.

BOOKS   MUSIC   FILMS

WEB   ART   OTHER

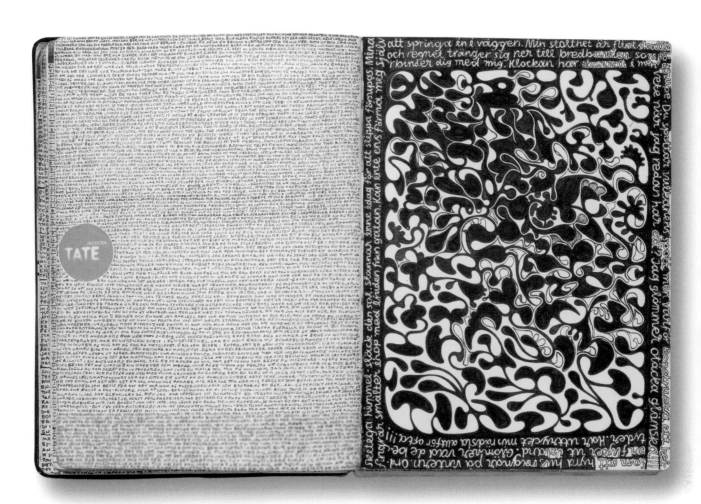

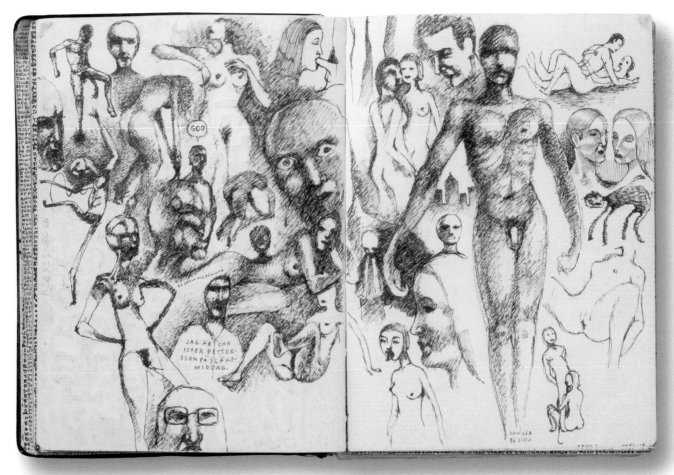

Faile is a New York-based trio: Aiko Nakagawa from Japan, Patrick McNeil from Canada and Patrick Miller from the US were united by the idea of an art collective – similar to a band – but as visual artists. "Our process of creating work involves synthesizing images to create visually visceral experiences, very similar to the way a DJ samples beats to create an audible experience."

Over the years Faile have pasted and painted the streets of New York, London, Paris, Amsterdam, Berlin, Barcelona, Copenhagen and Tokyo. They have published four books and exhibited in galleries across the US, Europe and Japan. They are currently exhibiting at the Baltic Center for the Arts, Newcastle, UK and Fifty 24 Space, Portland, USA.

info@faile.net

PMc: = Patrick McNeil
AN: = Aiko Nakagawa
PM: = Patrick Miller

Do you scribble into notebooks?
PMc: I work on scrap pieces of paper and keep the idea in my pocket until I do the idea or until I lose the piece of paper.
Do you use your work to exorcise elements from your life, or is work a hideout?
PM: I think it's an opportunity to touch something in yourself that you didn't know was there.
What's the most personal thing you'd be ready to share with others (well, us)?
AN: No comment.
PM: Sometimes I wake up in the middle of the night afraid.
That was interesting, thank you. Now what about the truth?
AN: No comment.
PM: It was...
How important is the vernacular in your work?
PMc: Really important, we express a lot threw words and type in our work. I just wish I could spell better.
AN: It is important, but not always. Sometimes I like to be quiet.
Do you carry a camera with you?
PM: I am typically the camera man. You rarely see pictures of me.
Do you stop in the middle of the street to make a note in your diary or take a picture?
PMc: No because I live in NYC and cars here don't stop for assholes taking notes in the middle of the street.
PM: Mental pictures. Mental Lists. I forget what's on them.
Do you take cameras and/or notebooks with you on holidays? What's the result like?
PMc: I am not allowed to touch the good camera any more.
Do you work or think about work during your holidays?
PMc: Don't tell my wife. Yes I do. I think about it a lot more than I should.
good though.
PM: It's pretty good. Mom was a schoolteacher.
Do you smoke?
PMc: Yup, but not cigarettes and not all the time.
How bad is your telephone bill?
PMc: It's better than my wife's.
How would one go about creating map of your imagination?
PMc: Start by drawing a strong straight line in pencil on white paper, then scribble the shit out of it till your fingers are tired, then spit on it and light it on fire and watch it burn out.

Above from top
'Monster Heart', 2006
'Burning Sin', 2006
'Perfect Vanity', 2006
(All 68 x 68 inches Acrylic on Canvas)

Date of completion: 2000 - 2006
Brief d escription of work submitted:
Our sketchbooks comprise a variety of
processes, experimentation, scribbles,
notes and memories. They are a way for us
to free associate, collage and produce work
in a stream-of-consciousness fashion. The
sketchbooks have always been a place to
explore personal ideas as well as a
playground for us to have a sort of
visual conversation.

PEN
tell em
what they wanna
Hear

HOT
DESIGN
for the
MASSES

David Foldvari was born in Budapest in 1973. He has lived and worked in London since 1986 and is represented by Big Active.

www.davidfoldvari.co.uk
www.bigactive.com

Where does the personal stop and the professional begin? How much of your work is drawn from life?
a) Personal stops when you're working for someone else. b) All of it.

Do you use your work to exorcise elements from your life, or is work a hideout?
Both. Exorcising elements from life leads to a comfortable hideout.

What's the most personal thing you'd be ready to share with others (well, us)?
I can show you a kidney stone I had six years ago if you like. I've still got it somewhere.

That was interesting, thank you. Now what about the truth?
You can't get much more personal than looking at something that used to grow inside my kidney.

How important is the vernacular in your work?
It keeps some of my work private. Private thoughts that I want to put into my work without shouting about them.

Do you stop in the middle of the street to make a note in your diary or take a picture? What kind of notes? What kind of pictures?
I photograph people, buildings, animals, writing on walls

Do you take cameras and/or notebooks with you on holidays? What's the result like?
Always. My photos are generally shit, but they are fine as references for my work. I blame my camera too often.

What's your ideal holiday?
I don't have one. I get bored on beaches, I hate the countryside. I like cities. Barcelona is always good, beach & city rolled into one. I also like mountains. I prefer to keep moving rather than fall asleep in the sun for weeks.

Do you write postcards?
Never, I'm crap

How good is your handwriting?
Shocking, like a degenerate.

How would one go about creating map of your imagination?
Make a box, put something bad in it and find your way out.

Sometimes diaries make you want to weep and laugh. Sometimes they make you cringe. Sometimes it's all that at the same time. What about yours?
Undecipherable, even to me.

Left from top

Record sleeve prototype

Editorial, detail

Book cover prototype, detail

Image for "Head Heart & Hips", detail

Title of work submitted:
Sketchbook scans & notebook scans
Date of completion:
Sketchbook pages 2004-2006
Notebook pages are 2005-2006

FRUIT

ILL.

INTRO — BEAT WITHOUT RIM
+
FLUTE 1

BREAK

FLUTE + ECHO

DROP 1

BEAT + RIM
BASS   WOBBLE   VARIATIONS

FLUTE 2   ECHOES

+
ADD

ACCEPT + PROCEED

ACCEPT + PROCEED

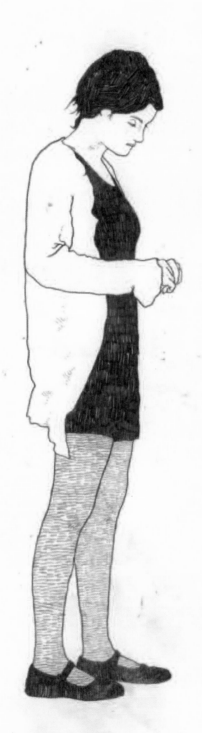

FAMILY
BUCKET

FAT WOMAN ✓
JOHN D.
CHILD MOLESTER — CHUD-MAN
ROY CHUBBY BROWN
ANIMAL — CAT / CAT LOVER?
DRINKING — LAGER LOUT?
STABBING?

090-095:
MASSIMO FRANCO

Born in 1972. Visited the
National Gallery in 1983. Visited
Rome with parents and saw
Michaelangelo's Sistine Chapel
in 1988. Moved to Glasgow and
studied drawing and painting in
1991. Took up a studio in Glasgow
in 1996. Awarded a period of
study at the Princes Drawing
School and commended by the BP
Awards in 2002. MA printmaking
course at Camberwell College of
Art in 2005. One-man show at
Cyril Gerber Fine Art, exhibited
at Eleven gallery, in 2006. Invited
by the V&A Museum to submit
a work for its collection.

*When do you look back? What do you do with
your old diaries and notebooks (apart from
submitting them to graphic)?*
Some I've exhibited, otherwise I keep them
in a drawers. I look back sometimes to see if
there's anything I can use in them for a picture
or another drawing or something I've written
that might help form part of an essay.
*Where does the personal stop and the
professional begin? How much of your work
is drawn from life?*
I draw from life most of the time. If I'm
not doing that, then it's usually from
reproductions of other artists work. I've
been reading Debuffet's ideas on Art Brut:
he believes that the art of the mentally ill –
because of their detachment from reality
i.e. the external – is forced into an internal
stratosphere which is entirely of its own.
The work they make is more personal as
they are unable to consider an audience.
*Do you use your work to exorcise elements
from your life, or is work a hideout?*
The writing can often be cathartic. The hidden
secret interests me.
*What do you have in your pockets when you
leave the house?*
Small change, Tesco clubcard, Tate
membership card, photocopy card, student
ID card, cash point card, diary, pencil, eraser,
pencil sharpener.
*Do you stop in the middle of the street to make
a note in your diary or take a picture? What
kind of notes? What kind of pictures?*
Yes I stop to make a note or to draw. I'll
put down an idea that might be useful for
something else or that is valid in its own
right and worth getting down. The drawings
mostly relate to people – it's the environment/
context that changes.
What's your ideal holiday?
Painting trip.
*Did you recall ever finding anything that
completely changed your work or your outlook
on something?*
Difficult question – we're always changing,
aren't we?
*Sometimes diaries make you want to weep
and laugh. Sometimes they make you cringe.
Sometimes it's all that at the same time.
What about yours?*
The writing often makes me cringe. As for
the imagery ... it's much more complex...
It's difficult to know.

Brief description of work submitted:

These are sketches made in small diaries. I've tried to grasp something immediate as opposed to being set on working to make a resolved/presentable drawing. I'm interested in the figure and this has led me to make drawings of people in the studio and other environments, such as out in the street, or in a shop, or other situations where you might see people acting in interesting ways.

Recent sketches made in life class involve the use of colour. This was refreshing after a period of using only monochrome and the arrival of Summer meant more opportunity to work in natural light as opposed to electric light. I enjoyed that a great deal

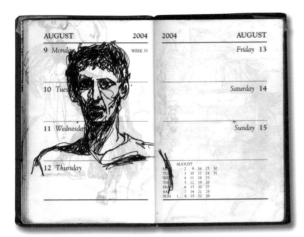

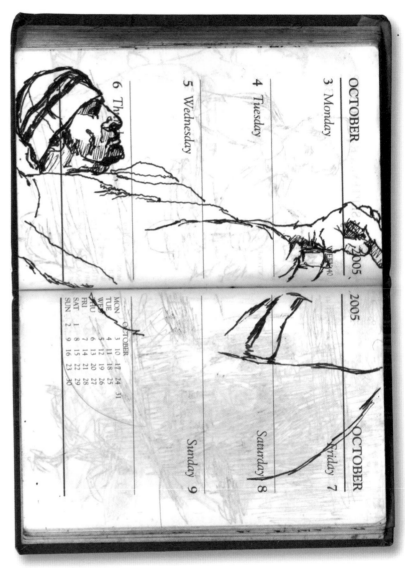

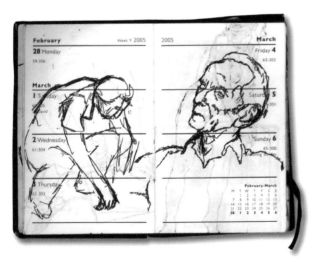

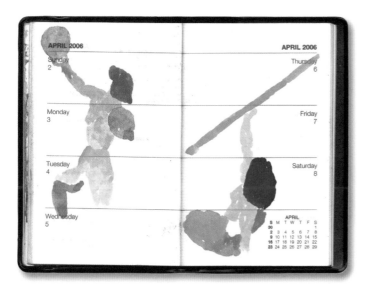

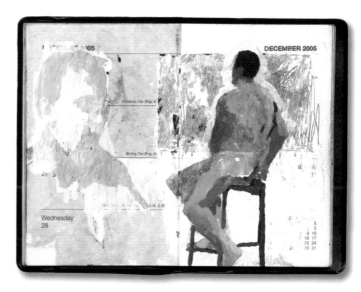

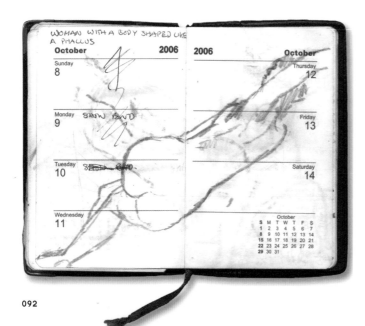

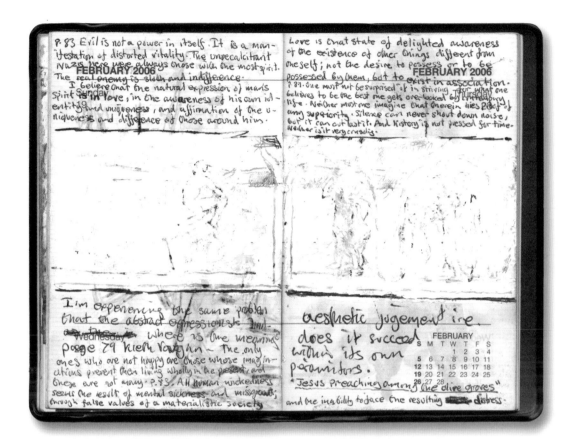

P. 83 Evil is not a power in itself. It is a man-ifestation of distorted vitality. The unrecalcitrant Nazis here were always those with the most spirit. The real enemy is sloth and indifference.

FEBRUARY 2006

Sunday

I believe that the natural expression of man's spirit is **in love**, in the awareness of his own id-entity and uniqueness, and affirmation of the u-niqueness and difference of those around him.

Wednesday

I'm experiencing the same problem that the abstract expressionists had — where is the meaning page 79 Keith Vaughan — The only ones who are not happy are those whose imagin-ations prevent then living wholly in the present, and these are not many. P. 85. All human wickedness seems the result of mental sickness and misgrowth; enough false values of a materialistic society

Love is that state of delighted awareness of the existence of other things different from oneself; not the desire to possess or to be possessed by them, but to exist in association.

FEBRUARY 2006

P. 89. One must not be surprised if in striving for what one believes to be the best one gets overlooked by the easy-going life. Neither must one imagine that therein lies proof of any superiority. Silence can never shout down noise, but it can out last it. And history is not pressed for time. Neither is it very crushing.

aesthetic judgement i.e.
does it succeed
within its own
parameters.

FEBRUARY

S	M	T	W	T	F	S
			1	2	3	4
5	6	7	8	9	10	11
12	13	14	15	16	17	18
19	20	21	22	23	24	25
26	27	28				

"Jesus preaching among the olive groves"
and the inability to face the resulting distress.

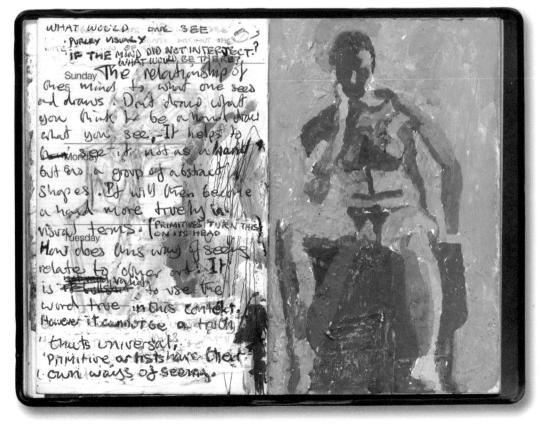

WHAT WOULD ONE SEE
PURELY VISUALY
IF THE MIND DID NOT INTERJECT?
WHAT WOULD BE THERE?

Sunday The relationship of ones mind to what one sees and draws. Don't draw what you think to be a hand draw what you see. It helps to

Monday see it not as a hand but as a group of abstract shapes. It will then become a hand more truely in visual terms. (PRIMITIVES TURN THIS ON ITS HEAD

Tuesday How does this way of seeing relate to 'other art'. It is valid to use the word true in this context. However it cannot be a truth thats universal, primitive artists have their own ways of seeing.

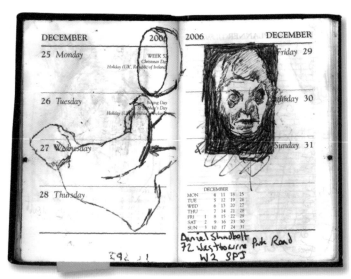

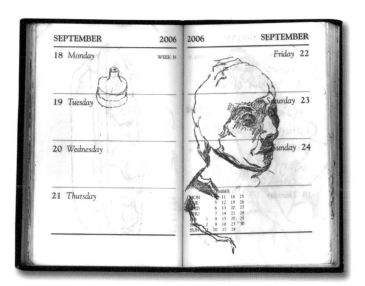

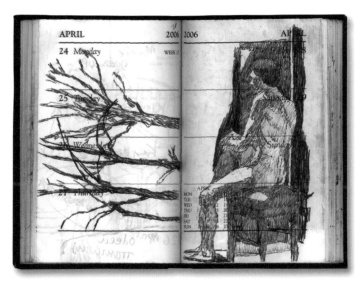

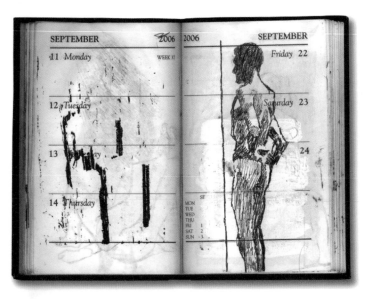

096-103:
JOHNNY HARDSTAFF

Johnny Hardstaff began his career in print graphics and eventually began to experiment with his own hybrid of graphic design and moving image. This led to his first 'film' *Phenomenon One*. Sony Playstation then commissioned the critically acclaimed *History of Gaming* from him. Signed to Black Dog Films, he worked with Radiohead and a series of high profile clients. Currently, Hardstaff is concentrating almost exclusively on his personal book and film projects.

www.johnnyhardstaff.com

When do you look back? What do you do with your old diaries and notebooks (apart from submitting them to graphic)?
Apart from the momentary pangs of embarrassment, what is interesting to see is just how much we change, how we mature and emerge from the blind fashion orientated nothing of our teens into hopefully more thoughtful, intelligent designers.
Where does the personal stop and the professional begin? How much of your work is drawn from life?
That's the battle. Keeping it personal in the face of, in spite of, in the midst of commercialism. Using corporate money to produce personal work.
Do you use your work to exorcise elements from your life, or is work a hideout?
Less a hideout than a sniper's foxhole, perhaps. I have a recurring dream: I am lying in a shallow trench / grave dug into forest floor. I have a rifle, and there are branches and bracken pulled across the top of the trench hiding my presence. As people walk above, stepping over me, I watch them through a peephole between the branches and then, when I'm ready, shoot them in the arse.
Do you write postcards?
No. I just don't feel the need to communicate with people I have purposefully gone away to have a break from.
Do you collect? What do you collect? Why?
I do have a minor collection of minor league sun-dried road kill and the like. Lizards, frogs etc. I like animal skulls and dead insects, the more exotic the better. The Japanese artist Ukawa Naohiro and I FedEx each other dead animals. I recently sent him a beautiful stoat skull. He has a rucksack sewn together from toads for me. The things I collect are triggers for ideas or aesthetics.
How would one go about creating map of your imagination?
You can't map it. Why would you? It's all we have separating us from 'them'.

Brief description of work submitted:
I don't keep a diary in the traditional sense, but that's of course exactly what my sketchbooks are. They're very uptight and retentive. Thousands and thousands of ideas crammed together. Often an idea will keep resurfacing throughout the pages, each time a little different until it's finally ready.

I know it's all in there: the shopping lists, names of people I fancied, people I both love and loathe, phone numbers, medical complaints, future plans now past, but it's all in there because they are just functional books for me.

If it's creative nudism, then frankly, I'm feeling adventurous. People can think they've got a handle on it, but it will always remain, at its deepest level, unintelligible to all but me. It's a language for one.

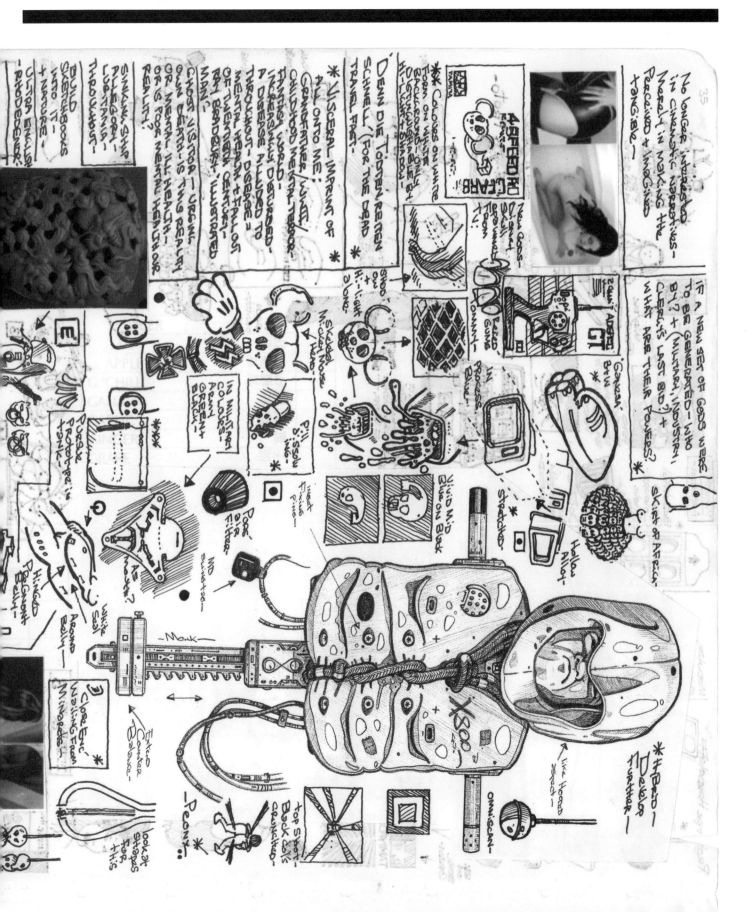

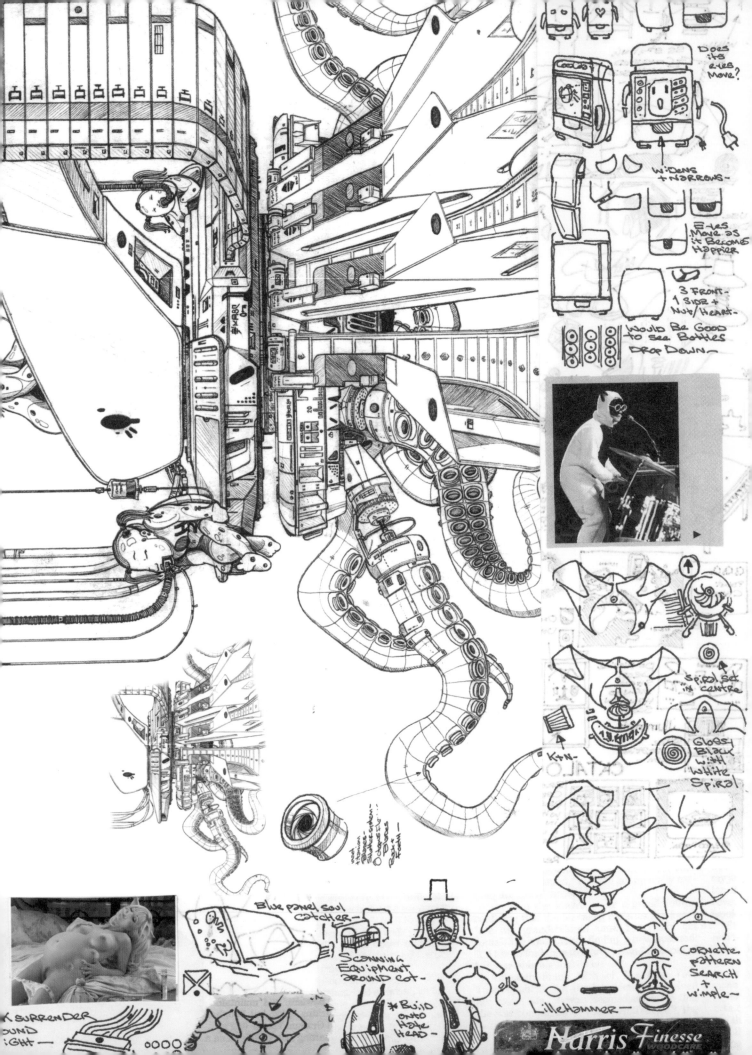

Does its eyes move?

Widens + Narrows —

Eyes Move as it Becomes Happier

3 Front – 1 Side + Nut/Heart —

Would Be Good to see Bottles Drop Down —

Spiral Set in centre

Glossy Black with White Spiral

K+N —

Blue panel soul catcher —

Scanning Equipment around cot —

Build onto Hare Head —

Cornette Pattern Search + Wimple —

Lillehammer —

Surrender ound ight —

Harris Finesse

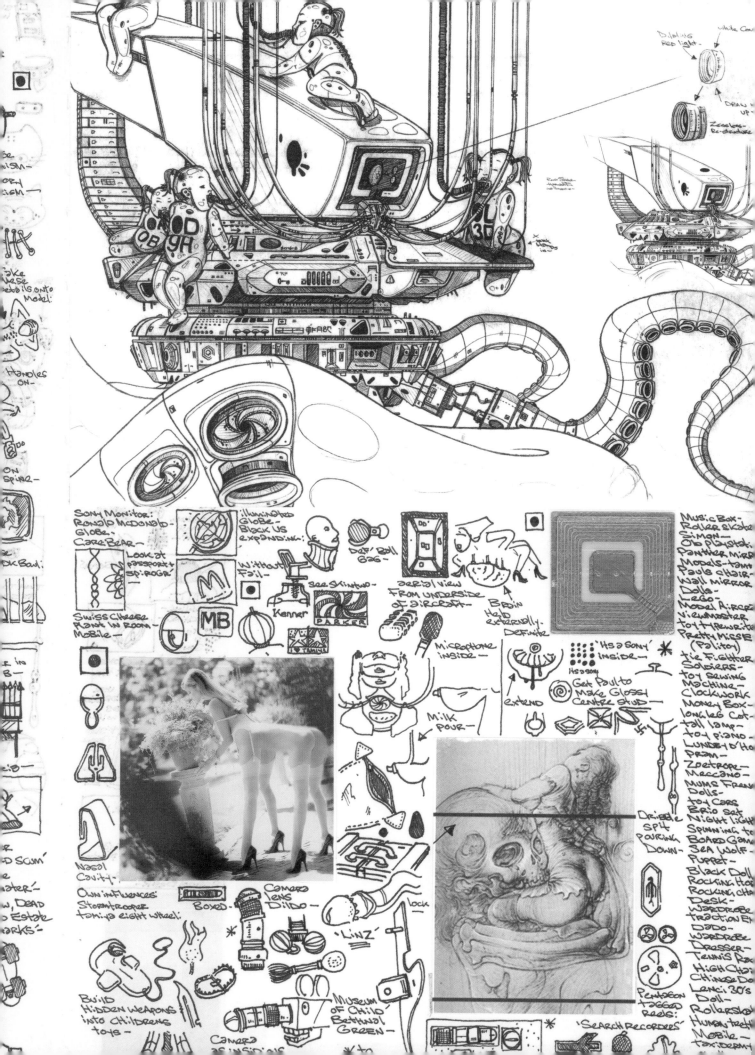

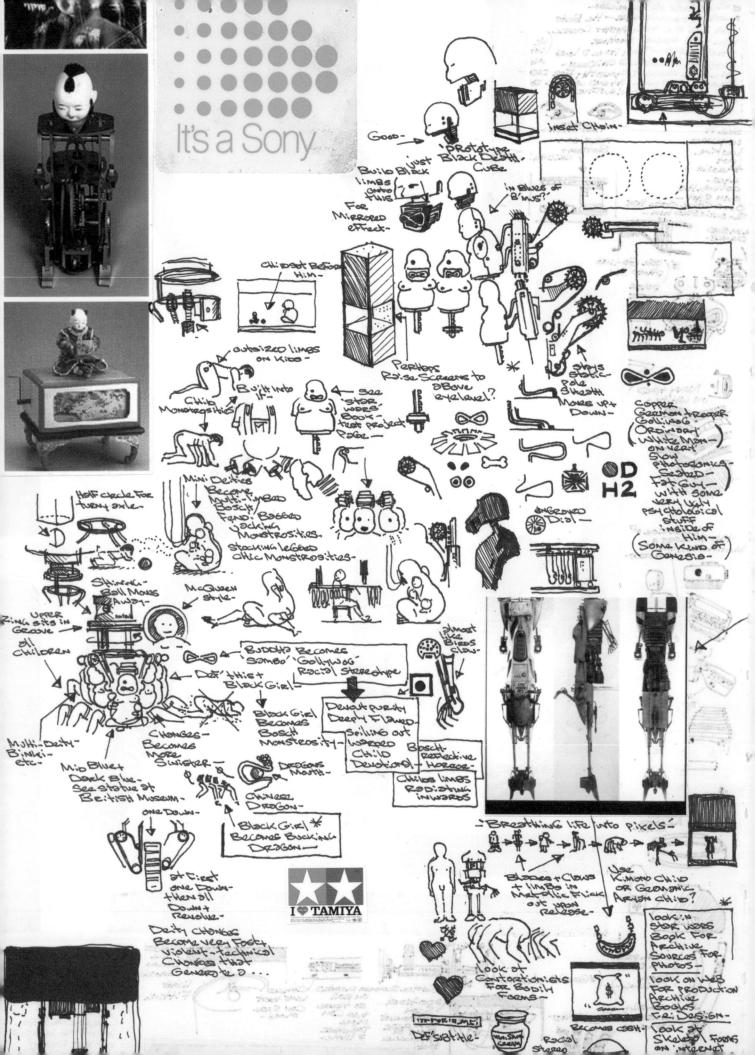

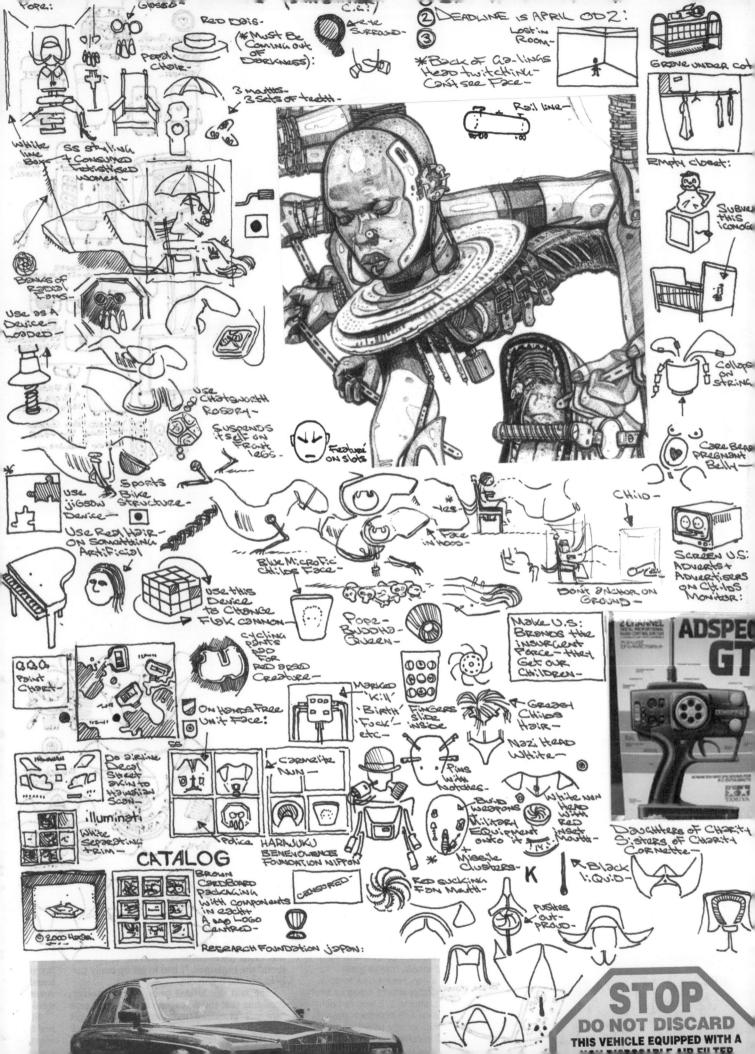

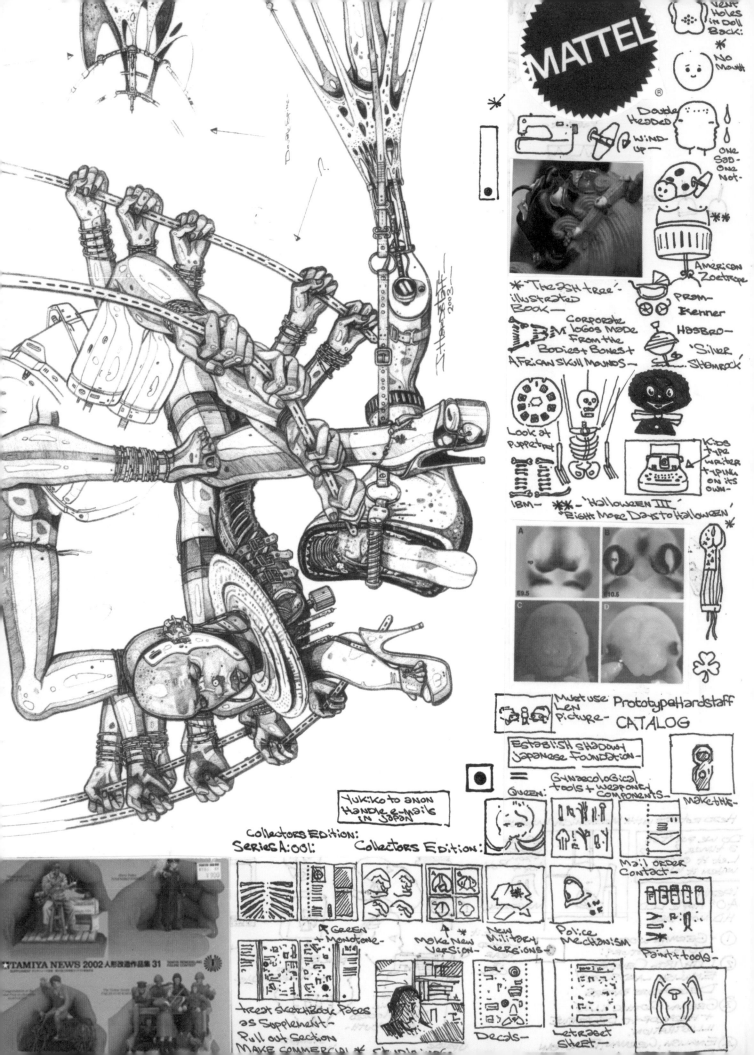

104-109:
IWANT

John Gilenson is a partner in the London creative agency iwant. Originally from a fine art background he moved into to design several years ago working in London and Prague. In 2003 he set up iwant with business partner Bruce Allaway. They specialize in brand identity, online viral campaigns, website design and art direction for wide variety of national and international clients.

www.iwantdesign.co.uk

Do you stop in the middle of the street to make a note in your diary or take a picture?
Not really on a day-to-day basis – only when I'm somewhere new or somewhere I don't often visit. Then I might take pictures of anything that catches my eye. Otherwise I use my phone to take snaps of anything that has an interesting style or use of type, colour – anything that looks fresh that gives me an idea.
How good is your handwriting?
Not good. It looks like a child's.
How bad is your telephone bill?
Not bad, I'm not too good on the phone.
How would one go about creating map of your imagination?
A large tracing-paper hat, some strong lighting and a biro would do the trick.
Sometimes diaries make you want to weep and laugh. Sometimes they make you cringe. Sometimes it's all that at the same time. What about yours?
My scribblings make me happy – anyone else would be confused and maybe a little bored.

This page
Clockwise from right
Typography for EBTG album cover
Buzzin Fly / Jimpster 12" artwork
Need2Soul 12" artwork

Title of work submitted (pages 106-109):
Every job everyday. Why we make what we make.

Brief description of work submitted:
The external image we attempt to portray and our internal desires have a common drive. Whatever head we wear on whatever day, our drives amount to the same, we want to make beautiful challenging exciting work that makes us proud, while at the same time we are always thinking of bigger better things and every job everyday we wonder whether that's the piece that gets noticed. Every job everyday.

This page
Clockwise from far left

Artwork for Chiltern St. Studios Invitation

Buzzin Fly Collage for flyer

Posters for Sound Transmitter tour

Electric Dr M & Spring Heel Jack flyer

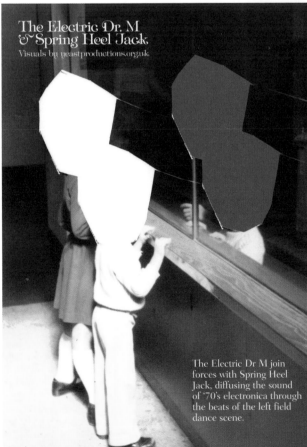

The Electric Dr M join forces with Spring Heel Jack, diffusing the sound of '70's electronica through the beats of the left field dance scene.

I WANT TO INSPIRE WITH ALL I MAKE

I WANT TO LOVE IS THAT OK?!!!

WHY DO YOU THINK THEY WILL

LIKE ME

CAN I

MAKE WHAT

I WANT

WHAT HAS

PROFANITY

GOT TO DO

WITH I AM

IT I WANT

I WANT

TO MATTER

BUT ITS

HARD

TO TELL

BE BETTER

ALWAYS THINKIN' GAME

I WANT

TO MAKE

A DIFFERENCE

2ND BUT ITS COOL I SMILE

SOMETHING

I

WANT

TO SEE

HOW OTHERS

DO IT

WHAT DO YOU

FEEL WHEN YOU LOOK

WHEN I WOKE THIS

I CAN SEE HIS IDEAS!!!

CALL THE WHOLE WORLD

I COULDN'T SLEEP AND I

THE BELIEF AND I

WHY WOULD YOU SAY YOU DON'T LIKE IT?

ITS DREAM

I WANTED TO

I WANT

TO HELP

WHEN THE TIME TO MAKE SOMETHING

I WANT YOU-WORK WITH ME TO WIN

I WANT YOU TO MAKE SOMETHING

WE CAN

ONLY

DO

OUR

BEST

WE ARE GOOD

DO MORNING

I AM

WE HAVE TO ACCEPT WE

AREN'T GOING TO WIN

EVERY PITCH

FUCK IT

I THINK

THEY'LL

COME

BACK!

Seb Jarnot has worked freelance for the last ten years. After collaborations with French magazines and newspapers such as, *Les Inrockuptibles*, *Coda*, *Libération*, he was commissioned by the French electronica label F Communications to create a series of record covers for artists such as Laurent Garnier, St Germain, Llorca, Manu Le Malin. In 2002 he worked with Wieden + Kennedy (Amsterdam) to create visuals for an international Nike print campaign.

In 2004, his own book *3x7=15* was published by Die Gestalten Verlag (Berlin). The book demonstrates the links between Seb's commissioned projects and his personal work.

www.sebjarnot.com

Where does the personal stop and the professional begin?
Both are getting muddled, I'm not sure it's very good. I work at home and the drawings I make to relax myself help me a lot professionally.

What do you have in your pockets when you leave the house?
A lighter and some money.

Do you carry a bag with you? Could you list the items inside it?
Yes I do, inside there are cigarettes, driving licence, three pens, a correction fluid pen, a sketchbook, my iPod, my mobile phone, various papers/flyers and my keys.

Do you stop in the middle of the street to make a note in your diary or take a picture? What kind of notes? What kind of pictures?
I often stop in the street when I see something interesting but I don't draw or take a picture, I look at the interesting thing and try to keep it in mind. And sometimes that comes back like a bubble in my head when I draw.

Do you collect? What do you collect?
I don't collect anything.

Did you recall ever finding anything that completely changed your work or your outlook on something?
A few years ago, I found a very cool bear made of clay and wool on a flea market I put it in my studio and it inspires me a lot.

How would one go about creating map of your imagination?
That's their problem.

Sometimes diaries make you want to weep and laugh. Sometimes they make you cringe. Sometimes it's all that at the same time. What about yours?
I feel like it's somebody else's drawings, indeed generally I don't remember making them, I only know I've made them.

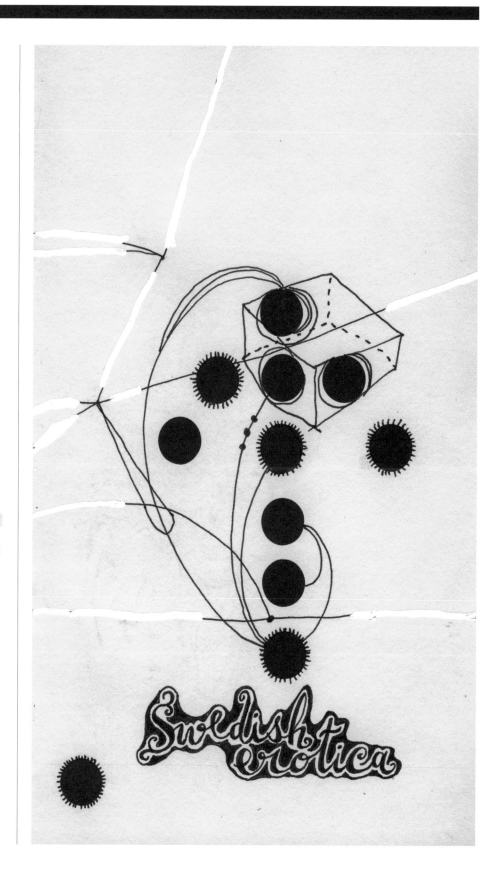

Brief description of work submitted:
I draw in sketchbooks on a regular basis. I'm very interested in drawing but I think what I do in my sketchbooks is closer to photography than illustration. I start directly with felt-tip without any plan. The result is always unexpected. I really like the idea of mental shooting sessions.

In this field of experimentation, I mix both intimate things and my graphic obsessions of the moment.

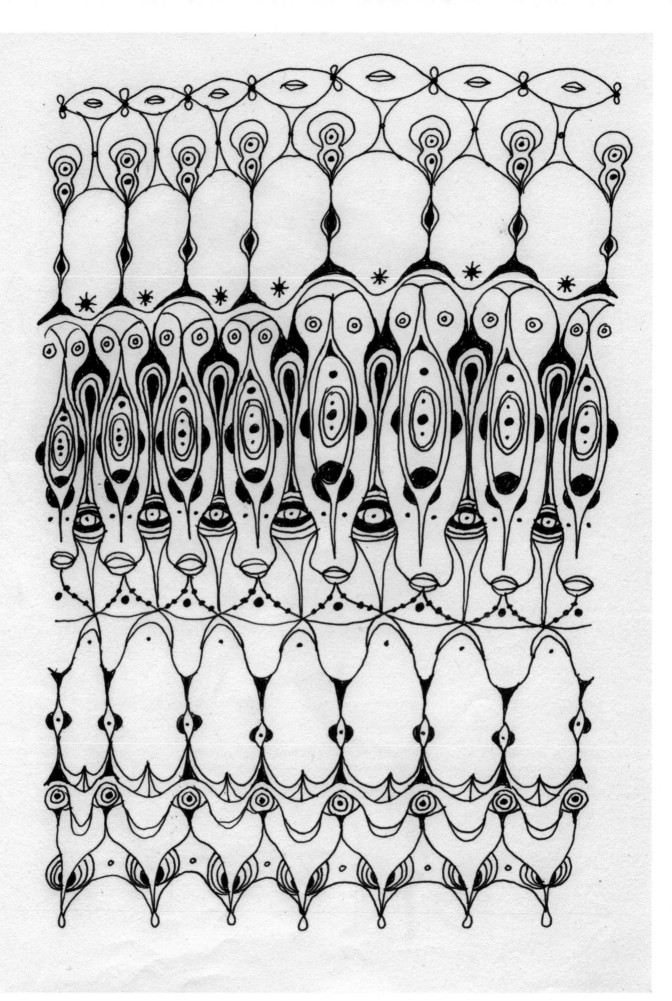

118–123:
TOM JUDD

Tom Judd studies at Manchester Metropolitan University and does freelance work for the BBC. In 2006 he set up the online community 5oup.com with his friend James Chambers to showcase student artists.

www.tomjuddeveryday.com
www.tomjudd.co.uk

Do you keep a diary? What kind of diary?
Not any more. One year was quite enough.
Do you scribble into notebooks? What about palm-pilots? Do you write for weblogs? Other? Why? How?
I always have a sketchbook on the go, which is where I vent everything and anything that is going on in my mind.
In terms of style, do you think 'personal' is a good thing?
Since finishing the year of drawing I have toned down the personal side of my work. It is still there but not as concentrated as it appeared in the pages of Everyday.
What's the most personal thing you'd be ready to share with others (well, us)?
I am left-handed.
That was interesting, thank you. Now what about the truth?
No really, I am.
Do you work or think about work during your holidays?
Last year I went to Corfu with my girlfriend. It was during my Everyday year so there was no getting away from it. I let her colour in sometimes when she got annoyed with my constant doodling.
How would one go about creating a map of your imagination?
They could start by looking through the 365 pages of Everyday, then give up.

From top

A self-promotional experiment using Photoshop.

I produced the front cover for my university magazine. It is hand-drawn then coloured in Photoshop.

An experimental piece combining vector and traditional techniques

Title of work submitted: Tom Judd's Everyday
Date of completion: 8 November 2005
Brief description of work submitted:
365 pages ago I had a very silly idea. Draw a page everyday for one year. Each day I spent around one hour on the page, sometimes more, sometimes less. There was never any planning or preparation, I would just go at it whenever I had a spare moment in my day and had something I needed to write or draw. Some of the drawings are observational and some are just plain weird. Monsters and things seem to crop up a lot (robots too). I have no explanation for this and don't care because its my book and I drew what ever I wanted on that particular day.

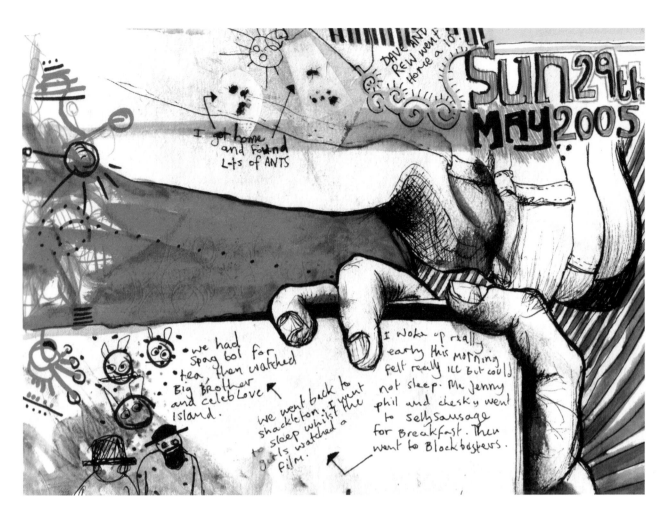

Hiro was born in Osaka Japan in 1980, and grew up in Tokyo and Chicago. He earned a BFA in illustration from Parsons, NY in 2004 and currently works as a freelance illustrator/artist in Brooklyn, NY. His artwork is inspired by various things including the Greek/Japanese myths, baseball cards and Bikuri-Man stickers. He is a garbage picker, specializing in construction woods and loves to paint over them.

www.shiloku.com
www.hirokurata.com
shiloku@gmail.com

Do you scribble into notebooks?
Yes, I do, but not for others. Just to organize my thoughts, or to have fun, or to kill time.
Are you honest with yourself on your diary?
Sometimes.
Where does the personal stop and the professional begin? How much of your work is drawn from life?
All of my work is not drawn from life, so there are no real borders between the work in my book and 'professional work'. But I often think that in my book I do more loose and experimental stuff, which leads me to new ideas.
What do you have in your pockets when you leave the house?
Lighter, change, camera (sometimes), my cigarette kit (OCB and filters!).
Do you carry a bag with you? Could you list the items inside it?
Black book, pen, iPod, extra hoodies for chilly nights.
How good is your handwriting?
Bad.
What do you collect?
Nothing.

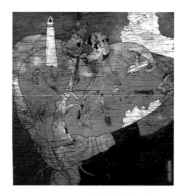

Above from top
'City with a big tree
'Greek Myth'
'Ny-Palestine'

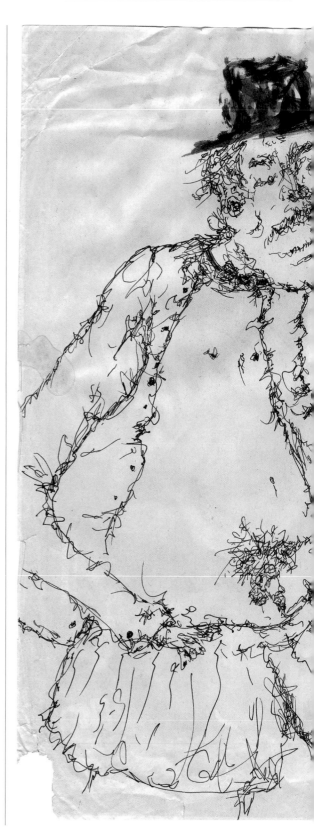

Title of work submitted:
Drawings of Hiro Kurata
Date of completion: 2003-2006
Brief description of work submitted:
These are pages from my sketchbooks and
notebooks, etc, of the past three years. I
bring my book to most of the places I go and
kill time with it, or let others hit my book.

So my books are filled with memories. I don't
usually go out and sketch what I see, but just
play around with some pens and thoughts.
One of my favourite mediums is the Pilot Hi-
tec 0.4 (in Europe it's called G-tec!), a brilliant
technological pen, and for the book, Canson
or Moleskine. Easy to carry, fits between your
butt and pants!

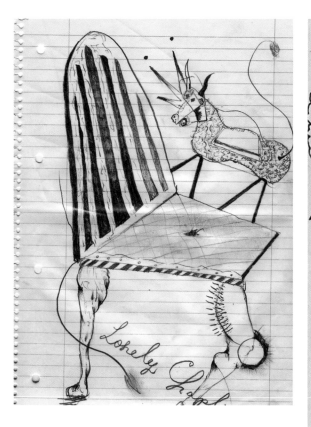

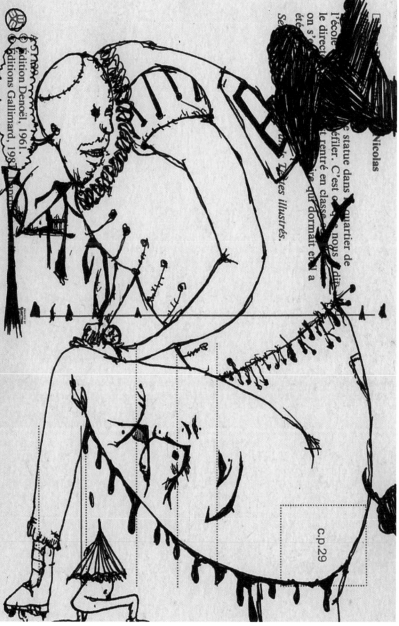

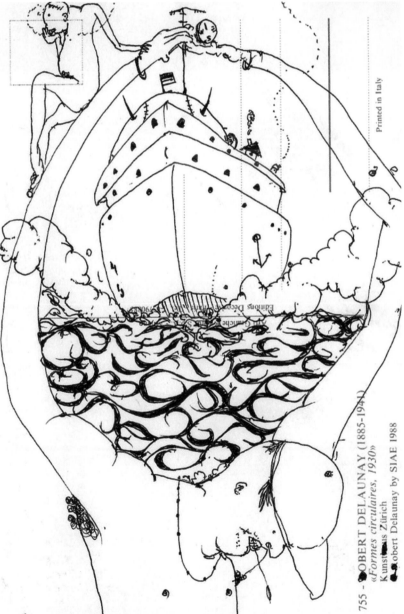

755 – ROBERT DELAUNAY (1885-1941)
«Formes circulaires, 1930»
Kunsthaus Zürich
● Robert Delaunay by SIAE 1988

Printed in Italy

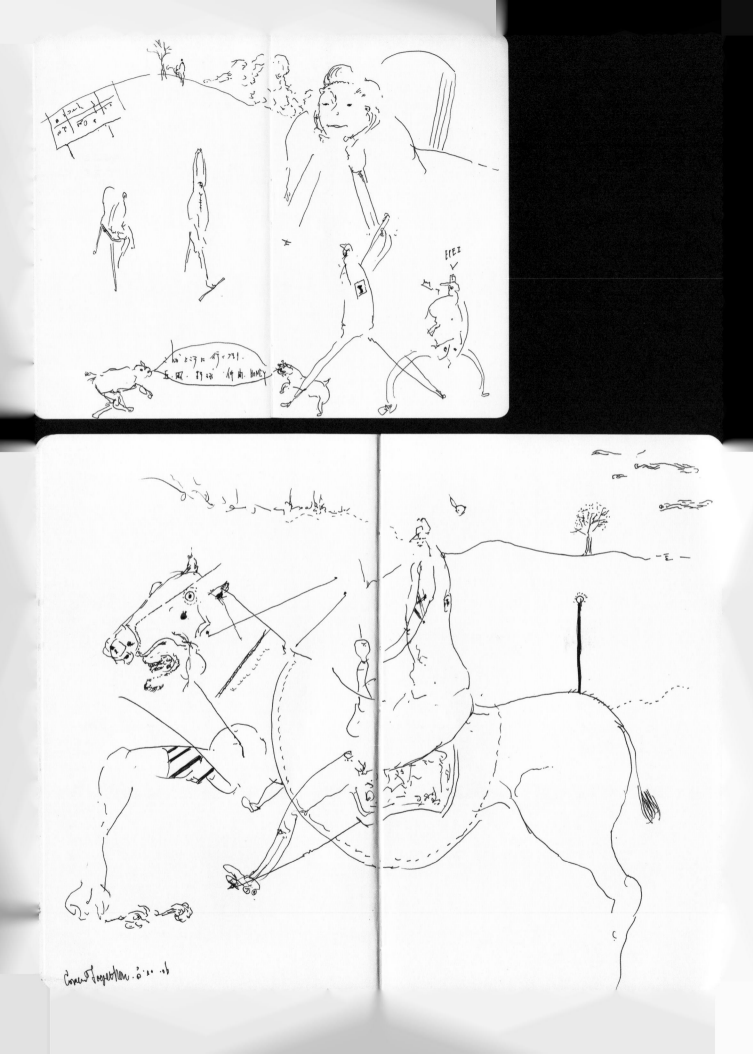

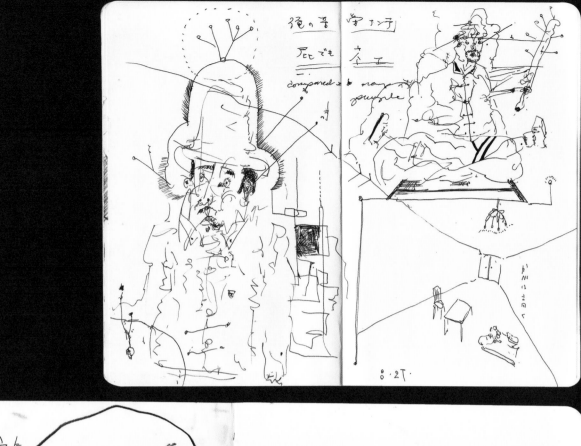

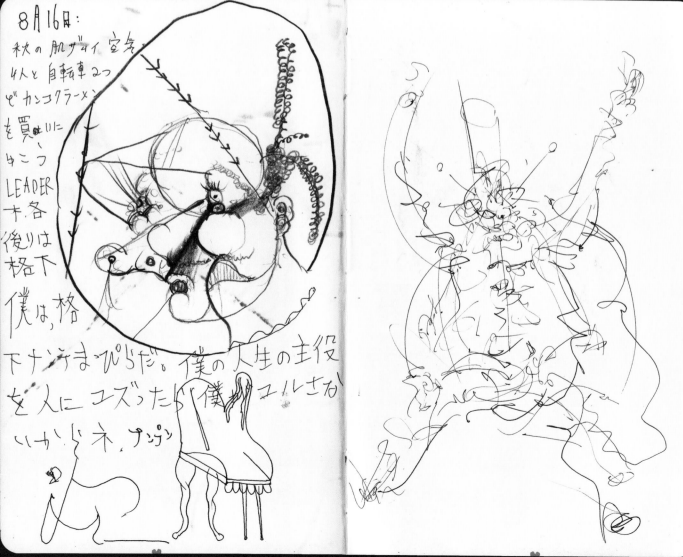

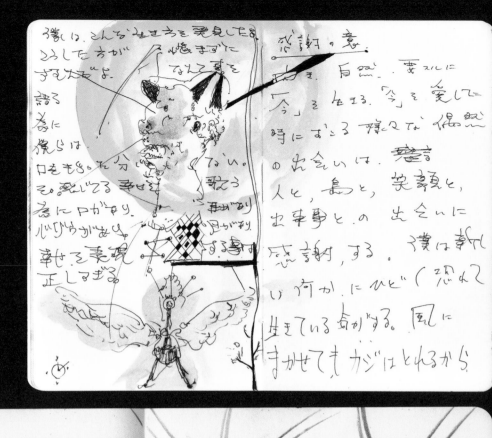

僕は、こんな生き方を発見した。
こうした方が 心休まずに
するんだよ。 なんて事を
語る
為に
僕らは
口をもった分。
そ 話してる 人に口がかり。
心らいらがあり
載せる素直
正しすぎる

感謝の意。

時き、自然。要スルに
「今」を生きる。「今」を美して
時にをこる様々な偶然
の出会いは。結言
人と、島と、笑顔と、
出来事との出会いに
感謝、する。僕は新し
い 何かにひどく恐れて
生きている気がする。風に
まかせても カジはとれるから。

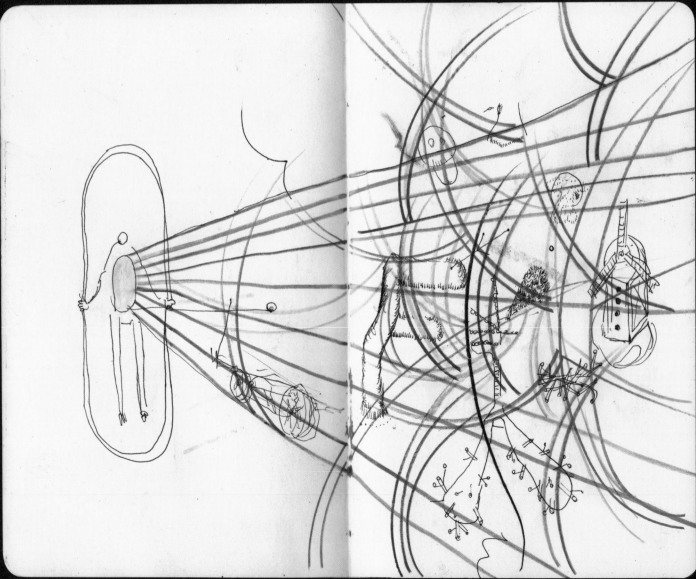

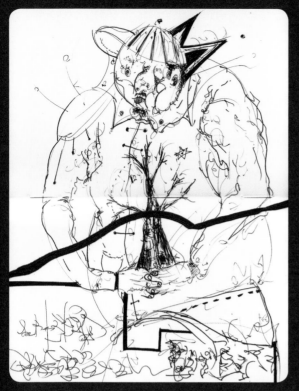

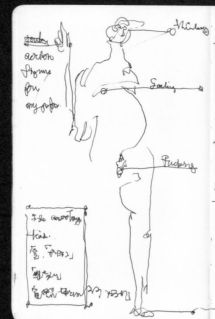

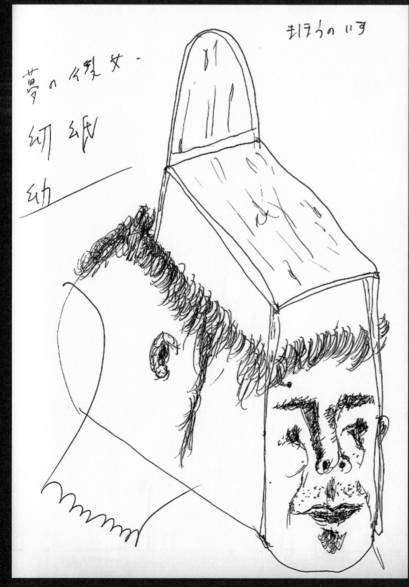

Florence Manlik (born 1967) lives in Paris. In 2000 she decided to move from a fine art background into illustration. She still works between the two disciplines but now her hand-drawn work has found its way into a broad range of products including books, CD covers, snowboards, clothing, packaging, shop windows and wallpaper.

www.manlik.blogspot.com

Above
Crop from personal diaries shown actual size

Do you keep a diary? What kind of diary?
Oh, yes. Keeping diaries is a strong addiction of mine.
When do you look back? What do you do with your old diaries and notebooks (apart from submitting them to graphic)?
Mostly when I need to, when my memory fails. When looking for my eight samples for you in all those diaries I felt a kind of nausea. It's all so soaked in the essence of me, a bit disgusting.
Do you use your work to exorcise elements from your life, or is work a hideout?
We'll need a psychoanalyst to answer that question. Anyway, what is the meaning of a represented thing/object/figure in an artwork? It could be that they are a symbol, a projection of anything else...
Do you stop in the middle of the street to make a note in your diary or take a picture? What kind of notes? What kind of pictures?
It happens. Some sentence running through my head or stolen from someone passing by, a picture of a hamster reading a newspaper...
Do you take cameras and/or notebooks with you on holidays? What's the result like?
Yes. An eclectic collection of instants. It doesn't have to look nice, it's totally free. I like to have as much elements as possible, to be able to reconstruct the events mentally, once they are already past.
How good is your handwriting?
Average. But I can write backwards and inversed.
Do you collect? What do you collect? Why?
No, not really, except the feathers my bird looses when molting.
Did you recall ever finding anything that completely changed your work or your outlook on something?
No, my evolution is quiet even if my outlook on things is unstable.
How would one go about creating map of your imagination?
Maybe he or she would be disappointed, finding only an immaterial blurb in there. I would disapprove of such a project, because they would probably get lost.

Title of work submitted: US diary
Date of completion: June 2006
Brief description of work submitted:
The idea behind my US diary was to send it out to the people we met during our very artistic journey through America, from may 19th until June the 4th. 2006. Four days in NYC, and then 10 days by car. It was quite a short time to drive all these miles and to see all the things we saw, but still enough to keep a micro diary, to take pictures, and to film. Once back in Paris with all that visual material I started to make this Grand diary. Voilà!

About technique: Dots are my newest passion. It is like being in a anterior state of drawing, even before the invention of the line. Time gets a substance, and things look like air, or powder, everything is floating, unreal, sparkling, passing.

L.A.

Wed. may 31st. vacance's day!! Carolina picked us up in the morning, Gillu was still a bit sick - did he catch my ex-cold? - but gava, and all three of us had breakfast on sunset bl 3900 w in the sun, fruits, coffee! Just great. she told us that Momus tried so hard once after one of his shows, but he failed ... in this attempt of what we could call "déjaponisation try", funny! Gillu bought a leather bag -best leather bags of L.A... men, brown & warm color, natural very nice, just i cité of the terrace where we stayed for a while.
Silver Lake
Echo Park
Chinatown i got myself bracelets
Bunker Hill (where John Fante lived)
Geffen's moca, gary's philарmonic buildings, downtown. We visited the puets hotel with pool on the roof, beautiful organs in the basement Gillu stayed on, but the staff wasn't enchanté by this music but we gas brave.

i really felt in love with L.A here for a while, hopefully we can come to live here for a while, someday - so relaxed, the city's display, the people, lifestyle ... all the reasons we talked to were friendly, a really good atmosphere houses, i were in those areas we visited, or maybe ... at least in those we felt so good to drive around it was because with Carolina, her music, the in a jaguar, where we had lunch, and then a swimm in Roosevelt, fact she was wearing gloves... we went to Little Tokyo, on the street. then i could have a football play on the grass field pool, outside, in the evening sun, chatting with Carolina while Gillu was filming, he could see it from our room 326. and then being watered, he could see it from our room 326. and then we went to Marina del Rei. to visit Juan on his boat. he's living on it, rents it like a flat. His friend Miguel was there too, it was calm & peaceful. Juan looks like a captain, but he never left the wharf, he ignores everything about sailing. he's just looks like this capitain / movies makes trailers, in things like this "fashion" distroute in Chino, must more the fashion distroute in Chino, must more in advertising / movies Miguel is 22, working Carolina & Juan both Mexican. they must have been travelling in both Mexican. about spicy food... we all had a nice breakfast and music.

Oh i forgot to write a few words about this man who was having oatmeal with his parrot called Minus. They both were enjoying their breakfast very naturaly, quietly. Minus didn't like me - i didn't take it personal, he just prefers men, it's all right, Minus! and this old man in his garden, in front of his house, with beautiful ferntree, who was adorable, really, it was a beautiful day. My very first time in Los Angeles. Enchantée. It was quite hard to say goodbye to Carolina when we got back to the hotel i spent 2 days together, and i really wish to keep in touch with this great person, miss Abonmrad! oh! i forgot aussi the wonderful old styre ice cream pistachio/ green tea we had before buying a necklace, what happend just before Marina del Rei, but voilà...

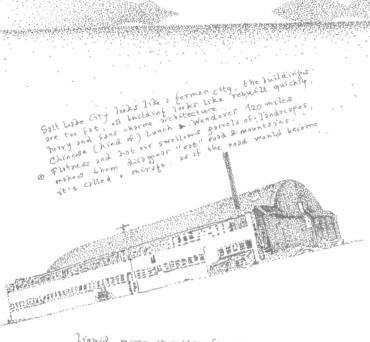

Salt Lake City looks like a german city, the buildings
are too fat, all building looks like rebuilt quickly,
heavy and sans charme architecture. Wendover 120 miles
Chinese (kind of) lunch ▶ Wendover 120 miles
⊙ Flatness and hot air swallows parcels of landscapes,
makes them disappear "eat" road & mountains.
it's called a mirage. as if the road would become

thu. june 1st
got up a 4:30 am, left the Roosevelt
at 5am to go to LAX airport, bye bye L.A!
→ Salt Lake City, airport, bye bye L.A
about 12-1pm, i'm waiting for my
personal gillu in the garage, he's trying
to get us another car that the one we had,
was given us by Alamo. we'd like to big-
same chore than the one we like to get
we love desolation, we love desolated
Buffalos and desolated salt flats; no, we
won't go in the mountain to olive mountain
bike, no, thank you sir. I hope we'll see
Buffalos, i never saw buffalos. we first are
going to have a lunch downtown Salt Lake City
and then we'll see the great Salt Lake (in which
we shouldn't swimm because it is too salty, and
if this salty water would went into eyes & noses,
we'd feel very sick.

Liquid, mirror or water. fascinating. we stopped at a salt lake.
sky blue, white, sky blue, striped landscape, magnificent, such
quiet, pure, strange, abstract. we walked, ran on the salt flats,
filmed a choreography, a salted choreography! drove on drove for
5 miles, very slowly but then the road ended, water flood over
the roads, we wouldn't be able to see the racing places.
the motel we were supposed to spend the night in was too miserable, we abandonned it and went to another day inn. some rest, sex,
shower, and then... surprise! on the top of the hill, huge
casinos— we're just on Nevada/utah's border — and on our left
handside, a very strange site, a disused camp, big buildings,
a display really looking like a deadcamp, concentration camp,

it was just the end of the day, darkness
was slowly coming, it really looked frightening,
but we felt attracted by the beauty of the huge
buildings, so we stood there for a while. strange
metallic noises were to hear, noone was really
around but quite near people lived in trailers.
Night came, and we felt hungry, so we had to go in the only
available restaurants were the casino's buffets! so we parked on
Montigo Boy weired parking and discovered this unexpected, surreal,
place, hallucinating casino, tousend times more crazy than Las Vegas's,
an indigestion of lights, colors, mirrors, patterns, just insane, impossible
to tell if beautiful or ugly, but after having been in the "dead camp", this
was just too much. Brainless place in the desolated surrounding.
Fri. june 2nd.

at plastic b. fast
at the hotel, little forgot
shopping - a last cassette
's camera! another reportage of the
dead camps! which is the place where
they put together Hiroshima's bomb - all
those broken windows, huge building areas
and beautiful, look so tragical, it's a mix
base, still a little in use, a plane took off
and then we drove to Antelope is
land to see the first buffalos of our
the 152
Buffalos
han not...

JFK 11:37pm. taxi, and
one hour later, we were sitting in
Karinchan's appartment, eating wonderful Karinko!
hot soba she cooked for us, tcho oichii! Karinko!
sat. june 3rd. breakfast deluxe at union square
with DeLuxe friends Gillu & Karinchan, rain beautiful
N.Y, i even got my jeans!! phillip and silver apple
cds at other music, and Karinko accompanied us to
the airport of ain, to fly back to Paris this time,
byby= Karinchan, hello Grizeth, hello Cageson,
hello the plants!

Sun. may 3rd, 9pm
Cageson's back home, thank you Grizeth
for nursing our bird while we travelled!
we pretty much enjoyed our artistic trip
through america!

i felt about comi-
ng time down of the
cactus forest hill, duck
or this slippery dust
and stony ground any,
how i got back to
the car, my orange juice
cup still in my hand, me
gillu was waiting for me

Phoenix looks huge, about 70 x 30 km
wide. we only saw it passing by and when losing our way
because of bad signalized detour later we stopped in small town
Wickenburg for a delicieux brocoli & cheese soup. Don't-ois would retire
with 80% discount on everything i owner mister Bonttois would be added how
soon. Wickenburg would grow soon 1000 houses would join Phoenix
do they do that without water? it's desertic amercon loves # i-thick & .-
some time. mister Bonttois said.
3.03. cm. &illuis driving again. wearing turquoise & t-thick & .-

SAHARA

easy arrival in las Vegas about 7 pm. found the
monster hotel checked in and got the 18th floor.
room 1888. great view out of the
hotels Buffet where i felt like in the pinocchio movie; fish, fish, green jelly
i loooove jelly. gerches ears, cake ; very nice quality food & service i las Vegas night life, crowd,
and sparkle. thousand lights drank huge margharitas went to venetos, Paris,
New York. we walked down the strip ± 6 km. watching Las Vegas night life, crowd,
places. thousand lights drank huge margharitas went to venetos, Paris,
cover version of another brick in the wall by the Pink Floyd,
volcano's eruption. it was fun.

Wynn.

shells hat, in this outfit he looked amusing
on a harley, a biker lady proposed him very
friendly to sitt in for a picture → perfect
touristic one ! - we head to Las Vegas on 60 w
which become 93 N so suddenly that we missed
it ... it's alright now, but we just hit
a poor bird, sorry, it must be dead
now sorry bird with the car/
6:30 SN become 5:30, Arizona - Nevada
2am, the great barrago food, at the Hoover
gillu & flo :

LES VACANCES
QUI ROULE PLUS VITE
QUE SON OMBRE

mon. may 29th - this is memorial day, a bank holiday, the
day for all veterans of all wars - these pratique 9:50 already
in the car at 8:45 in the desert again with traffic jam to
california, but so va / so va pas.
we drive to
San Diego

the performance;
we stopped at a gas station, to tank and
walk a little and then i discovered Billu's
hidden superpower! with the power of his
mind, yes, he could lift 2 tumble weeds and
project them far away or made them stay in the air
say with the tumble weeds, we were looking
for a good looking, typical tumble weed, those
you see in the moovie running through the screen
blown by strong wind, but for any reason they
weren't beige, but silver, and were entire bushes.
the idea was to send one tumble weed in a box
to Paris. it just wasn't the right type.
Then while Billu's went to make a phonecall
in San Diego who wrote on My Space, i started to clean all the A4 sheets of
paper that polluted the car's floors, for any reason Billu messed up with it had
quick look on the 2 or 3 first one, we didn't need anymore ok, and put them
all in the bin. i was very proud of my 'clean action' and drove us to San Diego.
But when arriving near the city, it appeared i'd been throwing our map about
to reach our hotel, in the trash. Merde! Billu was so angry! it took us about
1 hour, but we got there, i don't know, maybe due to Billu's new superpowers.

it was still possible to do Carolina,
which was planned with Carolina.
i mean to have a look the hundred
tousends of new building/houses,
the expanding of the city in the desert
- while also we saw a stephane couturier
photo exhibition of there san diego as is
looked so fantastic we thought could be first
a beautiful block 1988 Jaguar - she was driving
to see it for real - Carolina arrived with
with gloves on! - we met, and 5 minutes later
she was driving us to this area, she didn't see how
herself for many years and was astonished by how
it looks now ... it was only desert, hills when big
saw it last time, and now everywhere houses!
2 millions & monsoon ... it looked really beautiful!
those black houses in the sunset light, with the
black jaguar car. Carolina had also the opportunity
to assist another tumble weed experience, with even
bigger bushes. what a magic!   Carolina is 25,
born in Mexico, she half Mexican half Lebanese
and studying neurochimie at san diego's university
All together we went to a corean restaurant to have
nice noodle, and after the hotel, a demain!
so she drove us to the hotel.   MY BIRTHDAY
— tuesday may 30th.

— San Diego Zoo

ROOSEVELT

101

Carolina is member of the zoo; anyway,
we met quite early, she picked us up
and we went straight to see the pandas
on work & all water, earth & air creature in
the wonderful zoo's jungle. we were sup
posed to leave san diego fo fo to L.A. but
first we went to see the Salk institute, the
sea - the beach and then took Carolina to a
sushi terrassa for our last dejeuner together!
No! because i asked if she would like to come
to L.A, and she simply said yes! she's so
wild and free! we would go right after lunch,
and she would join us at about 9 PM, at the
Roosevelt - which became very chichi poopoo in the
meantime Billu was there when touring a few years
ago, it looked very different — soooo comfortable!
i was all agreeable with nice music from Carolina in the
to drive in 6 lines freeway /interstate! still don't know — roads without freaking out
pleasure. Los Angeles for the first time, my birthday! my very first donut ever, and in the
evening, at 101 diner, with Carolina and friend Juan, i got this magnificent chocolate brownie
with vanila ice 86   BIRTHDAY CAKE!

i was driving! Billu was a bit sick the
chevrolet, i was so proud being all
it was all
Thank you my new friends!

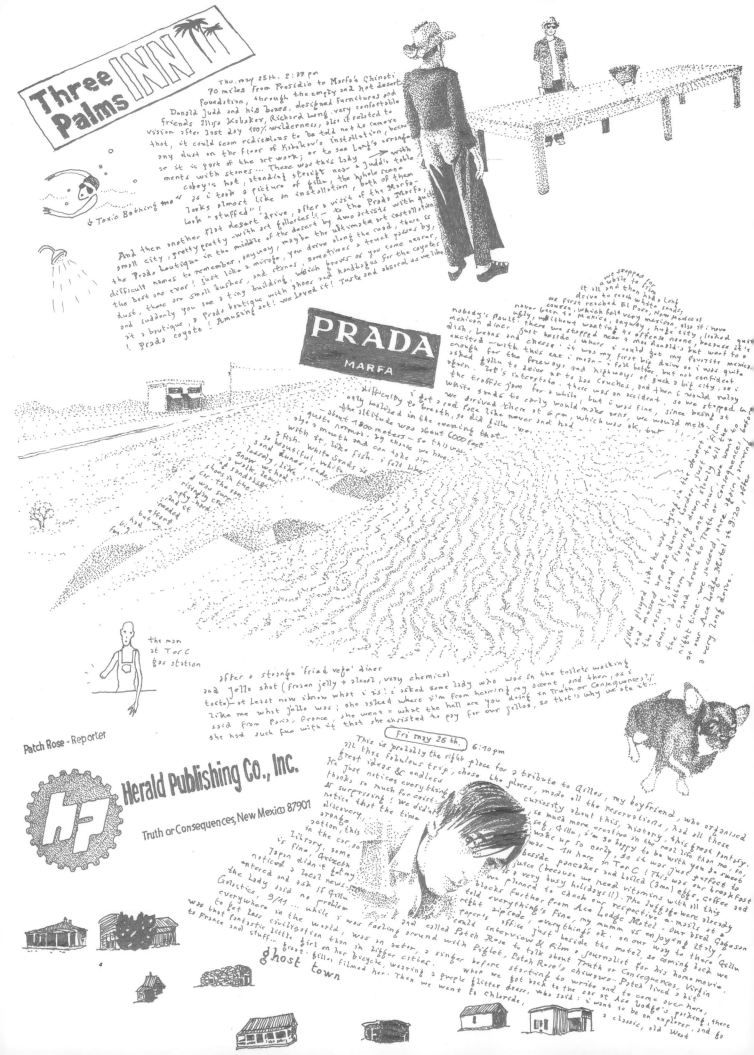

Three Palms INN

Thu. may 25th, 2:39 pm

70 miles from Presidio to Marfa's Chinoti Foundation, through the empty and hot desert. Donald Judd and his boxes, designed furnitures and friends Ilya Kabakov, Richard Long, very comfortable vision after last day 100% wilderness, also it related to that, it could seem ridiculous to be told not to remove any dust on the floor of Kabakov's installation, or to see Long's arrangements with stones... There was this lady - with cowboy's hat, standing straight near a Judd's table, the whole scene looks almost like an installation, both of them looks "stuffed"! as i took a picture of her, the Marfa, look "stuffed"!

And then another flat desert drive, after a visit of the Prada Marfa, small city, pretty pretty - with art galleries!! - to the Prada Boutique in the middle of the desert by two artists with quite difficult names to remember, anyway, maybe the ultimate art installation the best one ever! just like a mirage, you drive along the road, there is dust, there are small bushes, and stones, sometimes a truck passes by, and suddenly you see a tiny building, which brews or you come nearer, it a boutique, a Prada boutique with shoes and handbags for the coyotes! Prada coyote! Amusing art! we loved it! Taste and absurd as well like.

& Toxic Bathing mo...

the man at TorC Gas station

PRADA MARFA

we stopped for it all and then had a long drive to reach white sands, we first reached El Paco, New Mexico of course, which felt very mexican, also if i have never been to Mexico, anyway, huge city, looked quite ugly, without wanting to offense noone, because it's nobody's fault, there we stopped near a Mac Donald's but went to a mexican diner just beside i where i could get my favorite mexican dish, beans and cheese. it was my first big drive so i was quite excited - with this eat i mean - i felt better, but not confident enough for the freeway and highways of such a big city, so i asked Gollu to drive us to Las Cruches, and then a bit again. Let's interstate. there was an accident, so we stopped in the traffic jam for a while! but i was fine, since being at white sands too early would make sons, we would melt. we derived there at 6pm, which was ok, but i got a red face like never and had difficulty to breath, so did Gollu. we only realized in the evening that the altitude was about 6000 feet. about 1800 meters - so this was also normal. by chance we have quite a mouth and can take air with it, like fish. i felt like a fish. White Sands is so beautiful, white lovely like snow. we had a walk, leaving shoes in the and sandises. care the top rising crust. it was sur... nifly hard. and it effort... but 4... headed...

after a strange 'fried vefs' diner and Jello shot (frozen jelly + alcool, very chemical tacts) at least now i know what it is! i asked some lady who was in the toilets washing like me what Jello was, she asked where i'm from hearing my accent, and then, as i said from Paris, France, she went " what the hell are you doing in Truth or Consequences?," she had such fun with it that she insisted to pay for our Jellos, so that is why we ate it!!

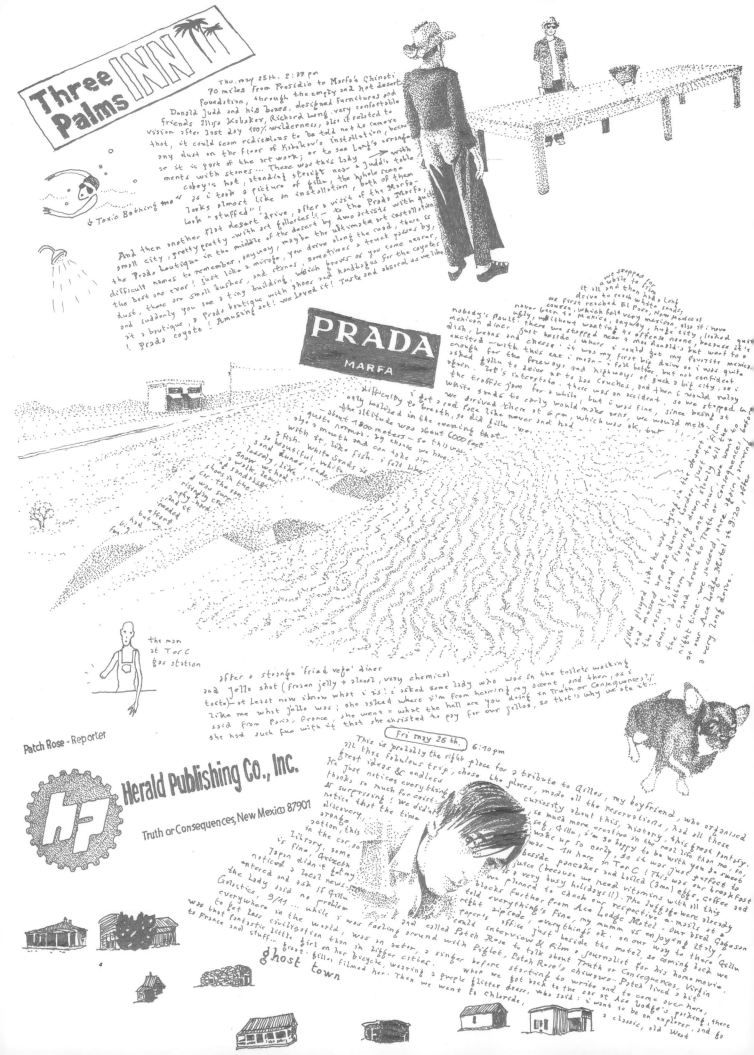

Patch Rose - Reporter

Herald Publishing Co., Inc.

Truth or Consequences, New Mexico 87901

Fri may 26 th. 6:10pm

This is probably the right place for a tribute to Gilles, my boyfriend, who organised all this fabulous trip, chose the places, made all the reservations, had all these great ideas & endless curiosity about this history, this great fantasy. He just notices everything, he is so much more creative in the real life than me, so thanks so much for exist! We didn't isabi & illa, i'm so happy to be with you so sweet surprising! We didn't notice that the time wake up so early, so it was just perfect to discovery, this was - 1H here in TorC! This was our breakfast action, this beside pancakes and boiled (3mn) eggs, coffee and in the car so a very busy holidays!!). The Judds were already blocks further from Ace Lodge Motel. Our used Gagosan library, some planned to check our respective e-mails at a is fine, Grizeth told everything's fine, my mumm is enjoyng 2&3/y, Gollu right zip code, everything ok. on our way to there Gollu entered and ask if Gollu office, just beside the motel, so coming back we Galactics 9/11 ... while i was fucking around with Piglet, Patch Rose to talk about Truth or Consequences, Virgin everywhere in the world, i was a actor, a singer before when we got back to the car at Ace Lodge's parking, there to get less civilization than in bigger cities. Patch lived a bit to France and stuff... little girl on her bicycle, wearing a purple glitter dress, who said : i want to be on explorer, and go Then we went to Chlorside, a classic, old West

ghost town

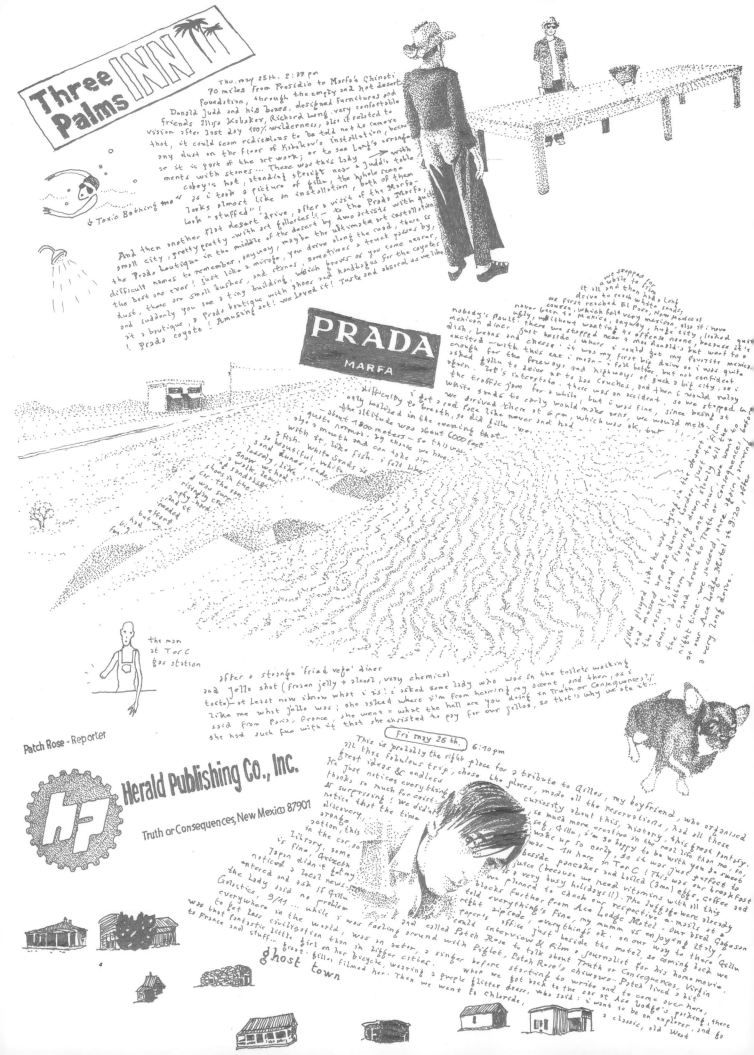

This is how some places in America looked like before 1900... some houses are still standing, the Edmunds family is taking care of the general store we could visit. there's also a saloon. Mrs Edmunds showed us, explaining over each single detail... we could see old tools, dresses, toys, a detonator – for the silvermines – so many objects & things the people used in their everyday lifes. Then, the idea was to take a grey (on the map) road instead of being back to TorC, which was 3 hours away, so we tried it out, but ended up on a dusty & stone road, it looked a bit dangerous to the wheels of our rental car, even at 10 miles/hour... there were 30 miles to drive. Luckily the only vehicule we met was a farmer & his son in a truck – both of them had incredibly blue eyes, turquoise! – the old man told the road and got any better., which was a shame, because of the time we could have saved, but also because it would have brought us directly to the observatory we saw on the map. mmh mmh, back to TorC, at least we could drive through the city's center, which we didn't made yet, and which was nice, with colorful house. TorC was called Hot Springs until 1950-60, but then it took the name of a TV program to get a show made in their town... there are still hot springs here.

Road road road, Socorro, on this route 60, straight straight line, fantastic road, and suddenly an extraordinary small town called Quemado where we had diner. walking to look for a phone Gillu discovered some shop with computer & office supplies mixed up with stuffed animals all covered with dust. it was to dark to film, but there were also those fantastic ghost stairs standing all alone next to the street... an art installation? we took some great pictures, but the resturant was incredible too, all well were covered with tree barks, trophees, old tools, animal trops... i still had stomac ache because of a hot dog we ate when leaving TorC at the gas station, so i had vegetables sticks and cottage cheese, it was just perfect, while Gillu had spagettis and a strange biscuit which didn't fit with spagetti i mean to me. maybe it is a traditional Quemado's way to make it. it was already dark, we continued our way to St. Johns, and on this road, we saw a sky, clear and full of stars, we never saw a sky like this before. we stopped twice to admire, fascinated. No wonder they placed there huge sky observatory in this county! we were 6000 feet high! we didn't realise why it was so difficult to breathe, why i had blood coming out of my nose, why our lips were so dry! Driving the car, we hit an animal – what was it? a little coyote? it seemed to be bigger than a rabbit, but smaller than a deer – poor animal, swimmassen, niee... hope it didn't suffer too much. i saw some rabbit's ears emerging off the grass, and a micro mouse crossed the road. finally we arrived in St Johns and stopped at our Days Inn motel. 50000 comfortable!

Sat. may 27th

after our breakfast we had a petite walk trough St. Johns, looking to the huge trees and the gardens and the cars, to see how people lives here and then let's go to the petrified forest & printed desert. trails, houses,

"i check up this petrified tree"

We checked up these petrified trees, 250 000 000 year old trunks which of stone became stone, marble. gigantic trunk made fully petrified, amazing... lying on the ground, we stopped to see some, drove through this national park, and enjoyed to see some very indian drawing engraved in huge blocs of rocks, and panorams of the printed hills standing in the dusty dry floor we enjoyed our discover after so much gigantisme, walking in the micro dry trees on crumble floor, like almost-dead bonsai under the heavy sun, fighting against the massive wind's assaults, still standing, ≈10cm high but so proud! in petrified boutique full of stones and fake indian souvenirs, and bought bracelets and things for our friends. in the cafeteria i could talk to a navajo Lodie, who explained to me what a "reservation" is. i thought it was a kind of zoo but not all, it's just a territory. we didn't go in an indian's reservation, but could see there were quite a lot in this area cause...

We had to go back to St. Johns so we stepped at the supermarket to get something to eat, there was a diner cheaper in the supermarket, i could have some water and then some cheese. then more it was almost to Tucson, i was getting more confident with... i drove us almost to Tucson, with this car, assure assure deucily... these landscapes, first still desertic becoming higher and higher as some how we had rock at the drowning, then they these kind of pins sticked into the ground this day! we had those cactus trees, Tucson's zero typical vegetation. Then Gillu drove...

Sun. may 28th

Because of our catastrophal arriving in Tucson i couldn't really appreciate the town, but we had quite a nice breakfast in a bagel place, and a promenade in a cactus forest by Botanica, looking like a food eye, handbag was looking for my night eye... these cactus but somehow in my right eye it was bone, reality, i must were about 6-10 meters high! when plucking this whole keep, we moved totaly carbly difficult was so scared out finally it was just... have put something in my eye, eyedrops helped.

140-145:
HANNA MELIN

Hanna Melin was born in Sweden. She moved to England to study and now lives in Hackney where she works as a freelance illustrator.

www.hannamelin.com
www.pvuk.com

In terms of style, do you think 'personal' is a good thing?
Absolutely. Isn't that the whole point of 'creativity'?

Do you use your work to exorcise elements from your life, or is work a hideout?
I used to do a lot of work involving personal issues. It was like therapy. But after a while I found myself looking for 'sad' things in my life (much better projects) and that made me depressed. Now I do more happy things.

Do you take cameras and/or notebooks with you on holidays? What's the result like?
I always bring my digital camera, and have about 20 photo albums filled with memories. They also work as a diary for me. I am not a good photographer, so I have become accomplished at editing by now.

Do you collect? What do you collect? Why?
I think in a way I collect memories. Old tickets, pens, shoes. etc.

How bad is your telephone bill?
I try to save money on that one at the moment. I email more than talk on the phone.

Sometimes diaries make you want to weep and laugh. Sometimes they make you cringe. Sometimes it's all that at the same time. What about yours?
There is a lot of cringe material in them. Especially from the early years when I thought I maybe should be a poet.

Clockwise from left

'I hate fancy dress parties'. Self-promotional work, 2006.

'Grandmother'. Image from grandmother's photo album, 2006

'DNA'. Illustration for La Habitacion, Barcelona, 2005

'Naked people in Cannes', 2005.
Observational drawing from beach in Cannes.

'Square dance is spreading like a virus'.
Illustration for Riot magazine, Amsterdam. 2006.

Title of work submitted: List
Date of completion: August 2006
Brief description of work submitted:
Every day I make lists of what I have to do.
I make lists because I am scared of forgetting.
They float around on loose paper, the back
of drawings or in my sketchbooks. I like the
feeling of completion when I can cross things
out. I add things throughout the day, so I
never manage to finish my lists. That's how
I have to have my day.

Today → Find lifejacket and cheese
Where is my funny hat? Book TAXI
TO STANSTEDT

Does the branch work?
BICYCLE HOUSE DINO
tuesday send invoice Print
out postcard postcard size
monday → sweden two/three
more books ~~today~~ THURSDAY
light → buy stamps selfportrait
Phone Sam write card. Get
food shirt outside today?
teapots make pricelist
do we need alcohol? FRIDAY →
Turtle blobs as outlines as
well ~~staffe~~ stair send
WEDNESDAY today bicycle
When is AOI? Exhibition
2 parrots Pay Bills Buy
PEN + HAT HEJDÅ

today → have a shower
Phone Inland Revenue
Find my wellington boots

monday Find my P60S

Buy CD → send pvuk send 3 adresses FIND corcscrew BANK → MONEY <u>monday</u> Phone Observer Print COWBOY Print **I LOVE YOU** ask ara if she got dreamweaver TODAY How much is a sewing machine chip crisps rabbits → BOOBTUBE **WEAR GREEN.** SEND INVOICE Buy black paper <u>mid**summer** → sill</u>

146-149: LUIS MENDO

Luis Mendo is a Spanish graphic designer living in Holland. After working in several studios for years he founded his own design company, Good Inc. While multidisciplinary, his main job is designing magazines.

www.goodinc.nl

Are you honest with yourself on your diary?
When I draw things for myself, I am, but never forget other people will probably see it so I am kind of cryptic about some things.
Where does the personal stop and the professional begin? How much of your work is drawn from life?
I don't think a good designer or artist can keep life and work separated. But the real inspiration comes from a good conversation with a weird guy in the streets.
In terms of style, do you think 'personal' is a good thing?
If by 'personal' you mean something intimate, close to yourself and honest, then it's definitely a good thing. Since the web became as big as it is today, many designers are copying each other all over the globe, so you get this very global style you see in graphics a lot today. It makes me sad to see this. I'm sure loads of young designers coming out today could be doing so much better if they look more inwards and less outwards.
What's the most personal thing you'd be ready to share with others (well, us)?
I am writing this in my pyjamas.
That was interesting, thank you. Now what about the truth?
I have this old Spanish book called *El difícil arte de la mentira* ('The difficult art of lying') written and drawn by Ceeseepe, and he explains how much more interesting the lie is, and how boring the truth. Now, what do you like to hear the most? I stick to lies.
How important is the vernacular in your work?
Important, but is almost invisible in my final work.
Do you work or think about work during your holidays?
Always. Don't you?
What's your ideal holiday?
No obligations, good weather, a couple of Moleskines.
Do you scribble on the margins of books?
Nope, I had an uptight education, I guess.
How good is your handwriting?
Less beautiful as I would like it to be.
Did you recall ever finding anything that completely changed your work or your outlook on something?
Having all those magazines in my aunt's place when I was a kid made me a magazine freak, I guess.
Sometimes diaries make you want to weep and laugh. Sometimes they make you cringe. Sometimes it's all that at the same time. What about yours?
I think mine aren't that moving. They are more a substitute for a terrible memory.

Above from top

ID, website, programme flyers and posters for Bibelot

left: Illustration for Blaadje
right: Cover of VPRO GIDS

ID and website for Dutch writer and newsreader Gijs Wanders

Title of work submitted: Selection from my diaries and sketchbooks
Date of completion: September 2006
Brief description of work submitted:
This is just a rough selection from my Moleskines. I keep them for work and for drawings. I can't keep the two separated, so there is a bit of everything.

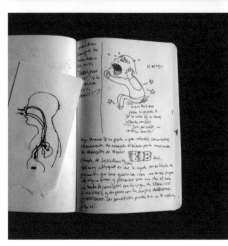

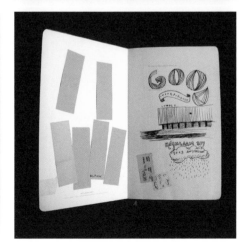

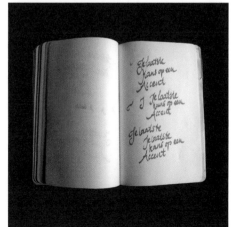

150-155:
KATE MOROSS

At the age of ten my mother told me: "In life, only do something that you are really hungry for". After foundation I discovered I was starving for one thing: graphic design. I began working for music promoters, labels and bands, designing anything I could get my hands on. I've since ventured out into film installation, photography projects and endless collaborations. Aged twenty, I am now studying for my degree at Camberwell.

kate@katemoross.com
www.katemoross.com

In terms of style, do you think 'personal' is a good thing?
With every project I try to create a unique style just for that client, which is certainly challenging. However, this is the only thing that makes your work grow.

Do you use your work to exorcise elements from your life, or is work a hideout?
At my best, I work normal hours and enjoy my evenings, but left to my own devices, I'm an insomniac workaholic.

Do you stop in the middle of the street to make a note in your diary or take a picture? What kind of notes? What kind of pictures?
Always taking pictures, it's easier than writing things down. I do write in a journal on the tube, careful not to look too much like an intense nerd or art kid.

Do you take cameras and/or notebooks with you on holidays?
Every holiday I start a new sketchbook. A fresh block of empty pages is always seductive.

Do you scribble on the margins of books?
Novels and non-paperbacks, yes. Post-it notes for art books.

How good is your handwriting?
I can be very anal about my handwriting. I have about 10 different kinds which use it in my work. I like full pages of closely written handwriting.

Do you collect? What do you collect? Why?
I collect zines, comics, records and T-shirts. Compared to the States, zines are quite hard to find in London.

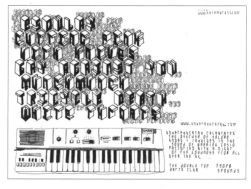

Above from top
Detail of illustration for the band Headless
Logo for Or Else
Detail from 'Love Hate' Book

Above from top
Flyer for Animal Collective
Flyer for Undereducated
Flyer for AA Concerts

Brief d escription of work submitted:
My sketchbooks and journals are filled with random sentences, scribbles and geeky library notes. They seem chaotic but some how among the pages there is some structure. I often scan the drawings from my journals, and put them side by side with client work on my website, I believe them to be just as important and an excellent example of the way in which I work.

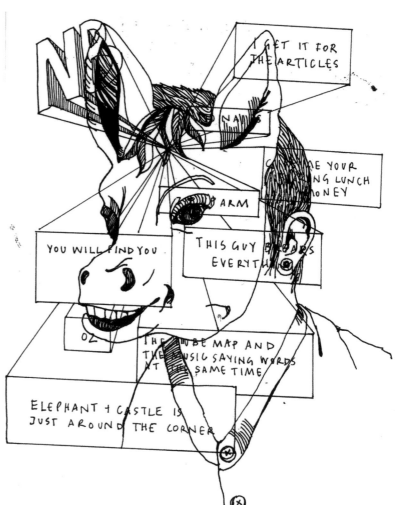

I LIKE BUYING THINGS

I LIKE BIRDS

TOM

IS SCARED

OF THE ROOF.

GEORGE DRAWS BAD DOG

HELMET

TREES

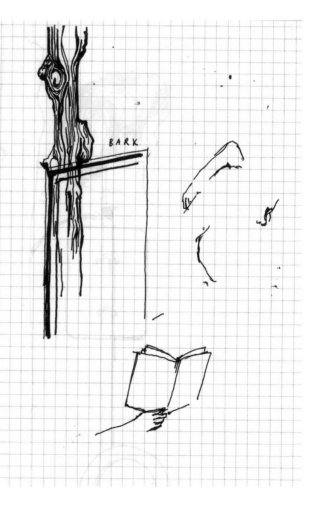

BARK

Originally from Philadelphia, Martha Rich lived a typical suburban life until she followed her husband to Los Angeles where, just short of a picket fence and 2.5 children, her average American life unravelled. To cope with divorce, fate lead her to an illustration class taught by the Clayton Brothers. They persuaded her to ditch the pantyhose world, quit her human resources job at Universal Studios and join the world of art. She graduated with honours from Art Center College of Design and is currently based in Pasadena obsessively painting undergarments, wigs, lobsters, and Loretta Lynn.

www.martharich.com

Are you honest with yourself on your diary?
Maybe. Depends. Sometimes self-deception gets you through the day.
In terms of style, do you think 'personal' is a good thing?
Yes. Not personal is boring.
What's the most personal thing you'd be ready to share with others (well, us)?
I used to repossess cars for a living and I was a girl scout until I was 13.
That was interesting, thank you. Now what about the truth?
The weight on my driver's license is a lie.
What do you have in your pockets when you leave the house?
Advil.
Do you carry a bag with you? Could you list the items inside it?
Yes, I am a girl. I feel anxious without my purse. Wallet, gum, money, pen, lipstick, camera, phone, old lottery ticket, crumbs.
Do you write postcards?
No, but I expect people to send them to me.
Do you collect?
I collect Frederick's of Hollywood catalogues from the sixties. Because they are excellent and hilarious.
Did you recall ever finding anything that completely changed your work or your outlook on something?
A 1965 Sears catalogue changed everything.

Above from top
'Wasted Ketchup'
'Tuff Enough'
'Backbone Such Fun'
'Bake Me Cake'

Brief description of work submitted:
'Weekend in Vegas', from my 2002 sketchbook.
The rest of the drawings are from my current
2006 sketchbooks. They were done on random
days and reflect random thoughts. I do
drawings while wasting time watching TV or
just piddling around my house. I don't usually
give them titles but if I must I would call them:

'Bad Wine'
'Don't be Fat or Ugly'
'Stop Talking Blow hard'
'Big Boob Club'
'TV Show Cry'
'Prom Night'
'Not Cool'
'Kicked Out'

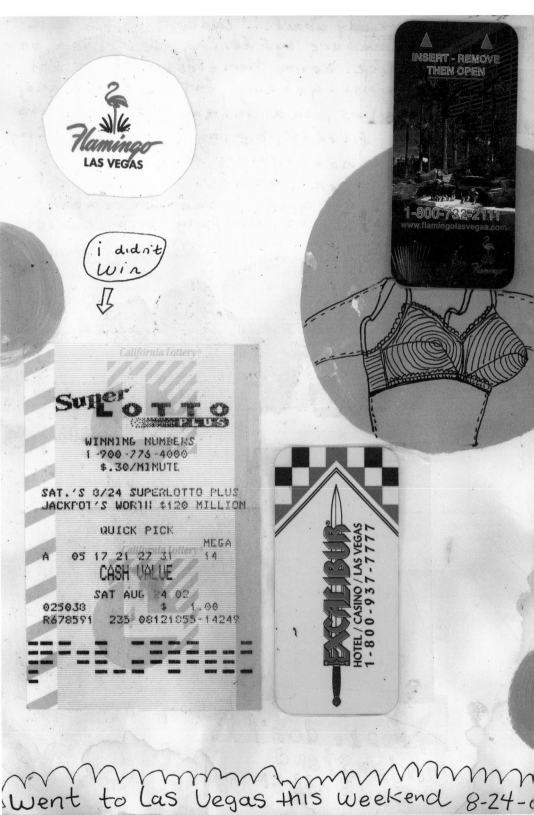

you are

A

BLOW

HARD

my lips are sealed

stop talking

I DO
Belong
TO
THE
BIG BOOB
CLUB

THESE DAYS I ONLY can cry during hospital TV shows

1/13/97

I HAVE BEEN ON A skateboard

Conversation with S. Growda

① He observed that quite often in pH range on the run sheet is too narrow eg 5.39 – 5.41 ie 5.4 ± 0.01 (cf license range of 5.4 ± 0.2). This presents him with difficulty when he does the validation. He has to a deviation of protocol & stay with licensed range

② Similarly they sometimes overshoot the alcohol concentration & add slightly more than needed

③ His commitments

kicked out

of

THE

LOVE

CLUB

166-171:
BARNABY RICHARDS

Barnaby Richards (born May 1974) is an illustrator and self-publisher. He grew up in Gloucestershire, Lebanon, Kuwait, London and Manchester before taking an MA in illustration at Falmouth College of Arts in Cornwall. His clients have included *The Independent*, *The Guardian*, *Dazed & Confused*, the Big Tomato Company, Paul Smith Jeans and Castrol. Barnaby self-publishes as Pending Press and is looking forward to unleashing a new series of *'Things'* books upon the unsuspecting public over the course of the following year. He currently resides in Frome, Somerset, living with his girlfriend Sophie. Sadly they have no pets.

www.barnabyrichards.co.uk
things@barnabyrichards.co.uk

In terms of style, do you think 'personal' is a good thing?
I think 'personal' is everything. Without it art becomes dull and interchangeable. It's a paradox that the more particular something is the more universal it can become.

What's the most personal thing you'd be ready to share with others (well, us)?
You know, unless you're Robert Lowell or something I tend to find confessional in art a little bit dull. You have to be really, really good to pull it off. Okay, I know that isn't exactly what your asking – and this is an interview not an artwork – but I think it is worth saying.

That was interesting, thank you. Now what about the truth?
Let me see... Two days ago I went to the dentist for the first time in over twenty years. I was terrified but it turned out to be not as bad as all that. Apart from anything else, she was cute.

Do you write postcards?
Yes. Banal greetings can be the provider of much comfort.

How good is your handwriting?
Very bad, I have to concentrate.

Do you collect? What do you collect? Why?
As a troubled teen I collected crucifixes. Nowadays it's mostly comics and illustrated books, the reasons being fairly obvious.

Do you recall ever finding anything that completely changed your work or your outlook on something?
Let me think of a good one... In my final year at university my dad sent me a copy of Andrzej Klimowski's '*The Depository*'. I immediately drew my own wordless story and soon after decided I wanted to be an illustrator.

Do you smoke?
Nope (used to – buckets!)

Below from top
Sketchbook pages

Title of work submitted (pages 168-171):
Here are some people who have inspired and influenced me
Date of completion: August 2006
Brief description of work submitted:
I had begun to fabricate a story about myself, the way I work and my inspiration, but it soon occurred to me that it wasn't really in the spirit of the brief. What *Graphic* wanted to see, I thought, was the behind-the-scenes. So I began to draw the footnotes: people who have inspired and influenced me. Of course, once you finish a project like this you invariably wonder 'why on earth did I forget to put so-and-so in' or 'does he really mean that much to me?' but the list was never meant to be definitive; just some famous people who have, to greater or lesser degree, meant something to me.

Clockwise from below

Detail from 'Devil Mountain'

Two illustrations for
'Children's Alphabet Mug'

Two triptychs from
'Agatha and the Perils of Love'
'Night'

Here are some famous people

Stevie Smith

Edward Gorey

Osamu Tezuka

Alfred Schnittke

Tom Waits

Leonard Cohen

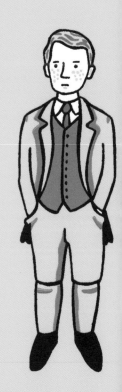

Edward Thoma

- writers, artists and musicians -

Guiseppe Penone

Jean de Brunhoff

Clifford Richards

MR James

Tove Jansson

Fernand Léger

Will Oldham

who have inspired and interested

Mimmo Paladino

Jesus

Dick Bruna

Charles Schulz

William Blake

Ursula le Guin

Ralph
Vaughan William

me over thirty-two years

Tomi Ungerer

Hergé

Maurice Ravel

amuel Palmer

Gram Parsons

Frans Masereel

Björk

Barnaby Richards

172–175:
REYNALDO VÁSQUEZ

Reynaldo Vásquez is a graphic artist by vocation and by need. While studying law he changed track and now works as an illustrator/animator based in Caracas, Venezuela.

hmto@hmto.net
www.hmto.net

When do you look back? What do you do with your old diaries and notebooks (apart from submitting them to graphic)?
I like to keep them because every piece of paper has an story, they are like a script of a movie.

What's the most personal thing you'd be ready to share with others (well, us)?
My notebooks.

That was interesting, thank you. Now what about the truth?
That is the truth.

What's your ideal holiday?
I like to travel with my girlfriend and my brother.

How good is your handwriting?
Good, I love calligraphy.

Do you collect? What do you collect? Why?
Yes, I collect notebooks and colour pencils. Because I like it and they're useful.

Did you recall ever finding anything that completely changed your work or your outlook on something?
When I dropped out of law school at 22.

How bad is your telephone bill?
It's normal, I only really use it to call my brother.

Above from top
Personal Postcard, 2006
Illustration for Faesthetic Magazine #6, 2006
Illustration for Bg Magazine #13, 2005
Illustration for Belio Magazine #18, 2005
Illustration for Platanoverde Magazine, 2006

Date of completion: 10 July 2006
Brief description of work submitted:
These illustrations are a selection of
my sketchbooks.

YO SOY UN HOMME MUITO FALIZ. MI MUJER ESTA MUERTA. LO MIO HIJITOS MA LO COMI AIER.
                              GAZIZZ

FANTAIZMA

[NAM-JUNE] PAIK MAN

SENIOR HELADO

176-181:
RYAN WALLACE

Ryan Wallace lives in Brooklyn, NY, and creates worlds of variously interpretable, often romanticist narratives. His pictures act autonomously and as a whole, each piece working as a segment lifted from a larger landscape or longer timeline. Recently, he has been shown in galleries in New York and California.

www.ryanmwallace.com

Do you keep a diary? What kind of diary?
Taking photographs is the closest thing that I do to keeping a diary. I will sometimes keep strings of emails if the dialogue seems worthwhile.

When do you look back? What do you do with your old diaries and notebooks (apart from submitting them to graphic)?
I look through old books and photos I've kept for ideas I have had and ideas I have forgotten.

In terms of style, do you think 'personal' is a good thing?
I think ideas are a good thing. I'm sceptical when style is the focus of discussion.

What do you have in your pockets when you leave the house?
Change, keys, wallet, nicotine gum, phone, portable music player.

Do you carry a bag with you? Could you list the items inside it?
Sometimes. If I have one, all of the above would be in said bag, plus books, magazines, receipts, bills, camera, sketchbook, drawing materials, lighter, planner, a note of foreign language phrases.

Do you work or think about work during your holidays?
Yes, but I'm getting better about this. It's a terrible habit. I'd much rather focus on swimming.

Do you write postcards?
Yes. I usual hand them to the recipients upon return though – which is another terrible habit.

Do you smoke?
Not right now.

Above from top
'Conduit of This and Adoration'
'In Celebration of Those Who Muster and Cut'
'In Celebration of Being Atop Again In Front of Everyone'
'Fear of Thieves Flying Close to the Surface of the Earth'
(All 2006)

Title of work submitted:
Conduits, Phugoids and Forests.
Date of completion: 2006
Brief description of work submitted:
Cut paper, Mylar and other collage elements in mixed media paintings. I keep this book on my studio table, and when I have excess paint around I'll apply it to the pages before leaving for the day, as a way of not completely wasting materials.

While creating the cut-out elements I paint over them in this book, leaving a stencil/rubbing. I also use it to reference palettes and colours that I may otherwise forget about. The pages create a kind of invisible layer that isn't seen in the finished work.

182–191:
SAGA WIDÉN

Saga Widen arrived in London from Sweden nine year ago. Still nostalgic for the calm of Swedish summers remembered long ago, Saga earns a living designing costumes for film, television, commercials and idents. She has written two books (so far confined in the drawer) and illustrated many, many stories written in her head.

www.sagawiden.com

Do you keep a diary? What kind of diary?
Yes, I've kept what I call an emotional diary since I was seven. It's mixed with fiction when I've found reality to hard to write.

Are you honest with yourself on your diary?
Very honest, when I write or draw it's for the moment and it's a dialog between me and myself.

What's the most personal thing you'd be ready to share?
Everything.

That was interesting, thank you. Now what about the truth?
I have got nothing to hide from people who don't know me, the truth makes no difference to them.

How important is the vernacular in your work?
I want people to relate to my work but they don't have to relate to it in my way or even know why I did it or what it means to me... Does that answer the question?

Do you carry a camera with you?
Sometimes, but my technical appliances rarely works.

What's your ideal holiday?
I would like to take the train and then the car. At this point in time I would avoid big cities going for great landscapes and small cities with great views and character full hotels. The food and the coffee would be good and the sky should be big and full of rain, and the sea should be stormy and I should watch it from the shore together with one other person.

Do you collect? What do you collect? Why?
Clothes, I guess. It's hell. I can't throw anything away because I love to dress and I never grow tired of anything as I find I can reuse and restyle things forever. I remember moments through clothes. I've tried to sell some, but now I tend to keep the summer wardrobe in storage in Sweden during the winter and exchange after seasons. I also collect porcelain bits that have been washed up on the beach by the summerhouse – I've done that since I was little. And round stones that I can make a wish on.

How bad is your telephone bill?
Very bad.

Brief description of work submitted:
I draw from what is around me, inside me.
I went to Sweden, stayed in the summerhouse
by the sea. Tried to stay out of emotional
trouble and clear my mind. Bernardo, an
Iranian young man with moustache, is a painter
and communist, he has almond shaped green
eyes and a Persian poppy tattooed on his arm.

One day a pigeon fell down an air vent
into a friend's kitchen. While still alive the
caretaker pulled it apart trying to get it out.
I couldn't stop thinking about it. To get ones
wings torn off.

192–199:
MATT WILLEY

Matt set up Studio8 Design with Zoë Bather after leaving his position as creative director of Frost design, London, in 2005.

www.studio8design.co.uk
info@studio8design.co.uk

Do you keep a diary? What kind of diary?
No, not in any conventional sense. I use sketchbooks but don't put the effort into them that I used to. I tend to scribble on anything to hand – beer mats, napkins, backs of menus, that kind of thing. Then I loose them.

Are you honest with yourself in your diary?
I write things down when I feel the need, which isn't very often (and usually when I'm drunk), and it's only ever for myself, so yes it is honest. I usually just write it down so it's there, so I've said it in some way. It's just a way of getting stuff out and putting it down. After that I'm not interested in keeping it. It would be intriguing to keep a diary because my memory is terrible, but I don't have the patience or the inclination.

Do you work or think about work during your holidays?
Yes, all the time, it's like an illness. I find it hard to switch off. I worry too much.

What's your ideal holiday?
With friends and family in rural France, lots of food and lots of wine. Or on a mountain somewhere (Appalachian mountains near Vermont would do) on my own, many many miles away from a phone or a computer... with lots of wine.

Do you write postcards?
No, I wish I was better at that. It's been my new years resolution for the last two years. Emails have replaced them these days and emails are crap. I get wonderful postcards from my dad. They're important to me.

How good is your handwriting?
Not great. It's hugely varied in direct correlation to how much coffee I have or haven't had. I often write things down which I then can't read. You should be able to read your own handwriting.

How would one go about creating a map of your imagination?
One wouldn't, it's a pointless idea.

From top
Spread from Zembla magazine issue#5
Spread from Zembla magazine issue#7
Spread from 'At This Rate' book
Spread from Royal Academy of Arts magazine

Title of work submitted:
Pages from a large green sketchbook
Date of completion:
From 1995 to 2006
Brief description of work submitted:
These are pages from an A3 sketchbook that
I've had for a long time. I doodle in it, stick
things in it and write in it.

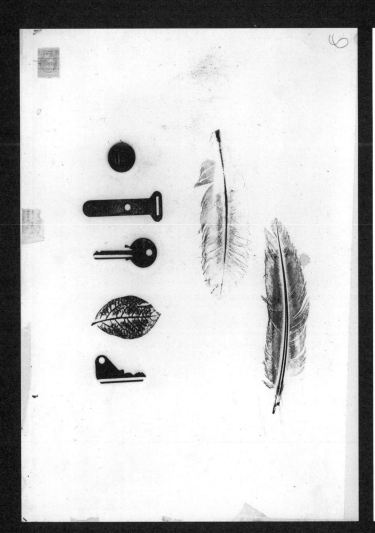

<u>heart</u> is simply a pump — the entire circuit of the blood going around ^through the
body tissues (~~systematic~~ systemic circulation) takes about 1 minute,
with the heart pumping around 5 to 7L (10-15 pints) of blood.
— Deoxygenated blood from the head & upper limbs pumps back into
the heart (down the Superior vena cava) ↑ meets the deoxygenated
blood being pumped up the Inferior vena cava from the trunk and lower
limbs — blood absorbs oxygen from both lungs and sends it back off
to the limbs etc. via the Aortic arch (upper limbs + head) &
Descending aorta (to trunk & lower limbs)

Tricuspid ring — Pulmonary ring
— Aortic ring
— Mitral ring
left ventricle — Right ventricle

<u>lungs</u>   2nd only to the heart in terms of work rate
↳ each lungs expands & contracts between
12 & 80 times a minute to supply the body
with oxygen & to expel carbon
dioxide ＊ <u>Swallowing</u> begins an involuntary process when food passes
from the mouth into the pharynx? Automatic reflexes take over to
control the subsequent stages of swallowing — muscles of the pharynx
contract & move food along → squeezing food along ustill it reaches the
top of the ~~way~~ oesophagus.

<u>Breathing</u> — vocal chords at the entrance ~~of~~ to the larynx
are relaxed & opened, creating a space
between them called the glottis

Pharynx
Larynx
Oesophagus

＊ swallowing
after the voluntary stage
of swallowing the passage
of food through the different
parts of the digestive
system is governed by
reflex actions
1. mouth — 1 minute
2. Oesophagus – 2-3 sec
3. Stomach 2 to 4 hours
4. Small intestine
   1 to 4 hours
5. Colon 10 hours to
   several days.

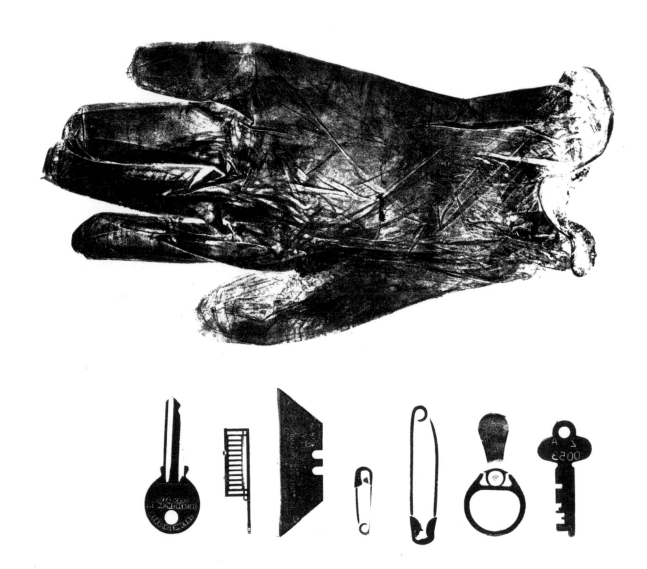

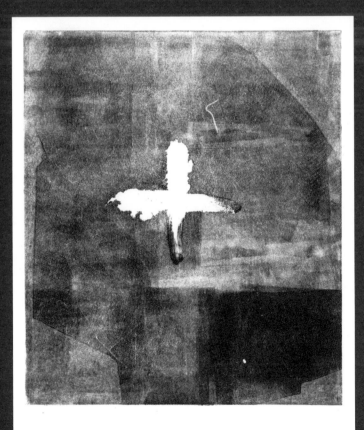
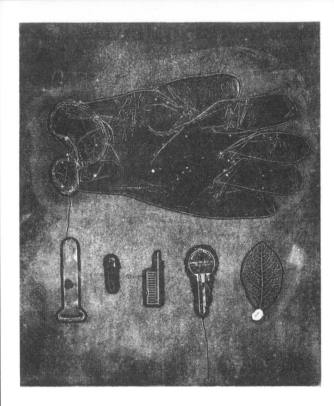

TYRES

K

'Notebook as relay'
An essay by **Dr. Stephen Bury**

"*I am for the art of fat truck-tyres and black eyes.*"
In addition to the recitation of a creed of such artistic beliefs, Claes Oldenburg's *Store Days* (1967) provides an inventory of his Lower East Side store's products – its plaster Statues of Liberty and Injun Souvenirs, scripts for the four performances or happenings that occurred in Oldenburg's Ray Gun Theater, drawings and photographs, diagrams and typescripts – concluding with a black-and-white photograph of a bath tub in a bare room, which probably influenced Anselm Kiefer's book *Hoffmann von Fallersleben auf Helgoland* (1980). *Store Days* is an artist's book, a Something Else Press book: it also a typical notebook/sketchbook – documenting, notating a present, projecting a future, where a small-scale 'unique multiple' will become a monumental sculpture, or providing a text for a performance which will mean something different at a future time and in a new context. The book contains within its 148 pages a greater, extendible world.

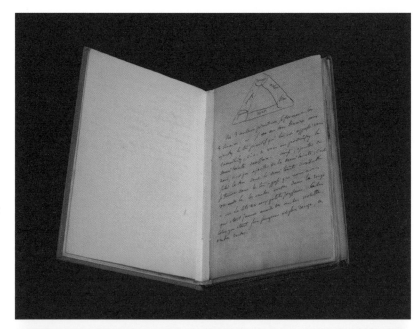

The artist's notebook is a creation of the Renaissance. Indeed, like the Academy, it is a notion bound up with the invention of the profession of artist. For example, Leonardo's notebooks conflate the interests of the *uomo universale*, the universal man, scientist and artist. Public interest in notebooks reflects its continuing obsession with the artist's touch (deemed to be particularly 'naked' in drawing and calligraphy), that chemistry of the finger tips in 'The Creation of Adam' from Michelangelo's Sistine ceiling.

The Romantic movement intensified this interest in proximity to the artist's or writer's idea, as if the notebook or sketch was – somehow – closer to the idea in the brain. This went with a fascination with the table talk of artists and writers, such as Hazlitt's conversations with the painter James Northcote – now institutionalised as the 'interview' – and also with an interest in the preliminary, the incomplete and the unfinished. Improved facsimile processes in the twentieth century made many sketchbooks and notebooks much more widely available – those of Turner, Delacroix, Ingres, Cezanne, Picasso, Marquet, Pollock etc. These would not only feed into art history but also back into art, as artists responded as if in some dialogue with their predecessors.

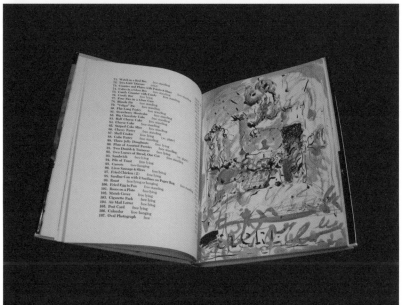

Today, in exhibitions of students' work notebooks and sketchbooks are often only available for the assessment, and then mysteriously disappear just before the public exhibition. It is assumed that the public does not want to see 'the workings', how the artist or designer got there. One could imagine a reversal, where the paintings, sculptures or film would be removed, leaving only the sketchbooks. Collaged, imperfect, inter-media – pen, pencil, watercolour, gouache, photograph, photocopy, realia, text and annotation - the notebook has the potential energy for future art. It is both research and a laboratory for the artist, graphic designer or illustrator.

It is documentation and explanation (and sometimes even deliberate obfuscation). It is a diary of dreams, Freudian condensation and compression. It is self-archiving, evidencing the results of experimentation and development. Although, for a student the sketchbook is never totally private, it has an aura of privacy, of freedom, where mistakes are not just permissible but encouraged. The book format, in its admittedly plodding seriality, allows a narrative to develop, however evasive the strategy the author may adopt: metonymic juxtaposition of text and text, text and image, image and text generates a desire for narrative closure. It is the blank paper before the blank canvas, and perhaps it is more forgiving.

Not that a notebook or sketchbook need be a book or always (over time) a book – it may exist in the artist's or designer's head, or like Tracy McKenna, who in her notebook, *Bulk* (1997), invites you to strew the 'perfectly bound' pages of London jottings – photographs, photographs of photographs, hand-written envelope notes, personal observations and bons mots – around the streets of London. It could be virtual - a computer file of digitally created and/or scanned content. It could be dispersed, mailed or e-mailed, texted or imaged, to others or oneself: we are in the era of the 'noteblog'.

But the notion of communication is important. And this is perhaps where the idea of relay comes in. I am using the term in the electrical sense, not least in the hope that an artist's or designer's sketchbook might have a kinetic value. It is a device where one circuit, often smaller, controls another circuit (and thus device) – a sort of switching mechanism. Translating this crudely, the notebook/sketchbook can switch on or off an area of art or design practice, a work of art. The relationship does not work the other way round: that is mere description or history. But the switching gear need not have anything to switch on. It is autonomous. The Italian futurist architect Sant'Elia produced a brilliant series of notebooks and prize entry sketches with their distinctly perspectively-distorted drawings – but only one ever resulted in an actual building – the Villa Elisi, Como (1912), a small hunting lodge for the industrialist, Romeo Longetti.

There are so many artists who have used diaries, notebooks, sketchbooks, photographs to 'relay' their ideas from time and place to other time and place – Daniel Spoerri's adjustment of descriptions of objects over time in the sequence of editions of *An Anecdoted Topography of Chance* (1966-), with accumulated dust on objects on the objects on his work table, or the linear addition to the artist's waistline; Richard Long; Hamish Fulton; Tracey Emin; Michael Landy; Lars Arrhenius; Fiona Banner, David Blamey etc. However, I will finish by briefly introducing four of my favourite notebook makers – that is, they appear frequently in my own notebooks and sketchbooks. I hope that this will give some flavour of the vitality across disciplines of their possibilities as 'relay'.

At the heart of romanticism is Samuel Taylor Coleridge, poet, journalist, lecturer and the philosopher who split 'fancy' from the 'imagination', to be taken up by T.E. Hulme in his formulation of British modernism. Coleridge's 'Christabel' notebooks of 1800 recount daytime and nighttime fell-walking with its panoramic descriptions and emotional calibrations of landscape and of fatherhood – the endpages are discoloured by rain and 'annotated', scribbled on, by his son, Hartley.

Marcel Duchamp with his almost secretive art practice, culminating in his posthumous installation, Etant donnés (1946-66), began publishing (some of the copies assembled by Joseph Cornell) La boîte en valise (1941-1966), a sort of portable museum of himself. After his death a collection of notes was published including remarks on *The Large Glass*. There is a sense of plan, of blueprint, in the spirit of Duchamp's move into art as the undisguised reflection of industrial and capitalist hegemony, not needing the disguise of 19th century iconography.

In his autobiography – a form of notation in itself – the Japanese film director Akira Kurosawa describes his lessons in calligraphy: 'in later years I was told by an older colleague in the movie world that "kuro-san's writing isn't writing, it's pictures."' His script books (and Kurosawa wrote many scripts for others both before and when he was a director) are virtuoso performances, and match the visuality of his films and their anchoring in text, so much so that one can overlook the rather everyday fact that the heavy rains in *Rashomon* and *The Seven Samurai* come from fire-hoses.

The notebook is a leitmotiv in Paul Auster's work. In 'City of Glass', the first story in the inter-related *New York Trilogy* (1985) – the detective Quinn, who assumes Auster's identity at the beginning of the story, carries a red notebook, whilst his 'suspect', the elder Stillman carries a smaller red notebook. Auster's own autobiographical *The Red Notebook* (1995) is a collage of personal reminiscence and various stories of coincidence and chance told him by friends and acquaintances. The notebook for Auster is both subject and object. It appears mise-en-abyme, a play within a play, a source of the narrative and embedded in it. This is perhaps the postmodern notebook.

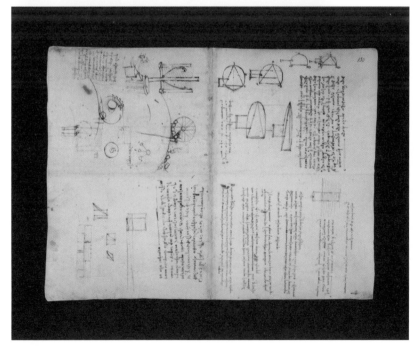

Opposite from top
Samuel Taylor Coleridge 'Notebooks' c.1808. © British Library Board
Claes Oldenburg 'Store Days', Something Else Press, 1967 © Claes Oldenburg
Eugene Delacroix 'Le Voyage de Eugène Delacroix au Maroc'. Facsimile album published in Paris, 1913

Above from top
Paul Auster 'The Red Notebook', Faber 1995. Cover photograph by The Douglas Brothers
Leonardo da Vinci 'Notebook' (Arundel 263) © British Library Board.

TWEED TWEED

My year of graphic design without ~~clients~~

After seven years of running a studio designing CD covers for Lou Reed, David Byrne and the Rolling Stones, I decided not to take on any ~~client~~ projects for a full year. On the surface, the year before had been the most successful to date, our designs had won gold medals from Warsaw to New York, from London to Moscow and the booming economy had filled our coffers. Underneath the surface, however, I was having less and less fun in the office. Work was getting mediocre and repetitive.

   I thought I really needed space to experiment and dream up bigger pictures. I wanted some room to re-evaluate what we were doing, decide what I wanted to say, indulge in work-intensive design obsessions for which there was not enough time during regular working times.

LEDEE LEDUM

by **Stefan Sagmeister**

During a workshop in Cranbrook I got envious of the students being able to just spend their whole waking hours experimenting. Then Ed Fella came to my studio in New York and showed off all his wonderful sketchbooks with free typographic experiments. That did it: I settled on a starting date of June 2000.

I wanted many people to know about my plan so I could not chicken out of it when June came around. I told our ~~clients~~ about it. They took it rather well, nobody was pissed-off, everybody seemed supportive. I had lunch with veteran designers Ivan Chermayeff and Tom Geismar from Chermayeff and Geismar, where Tom told me that they had been planning a similar move for the past 50 years.

My friend Chee Pearlman suggested I should keep a diary. Here it is:

JUNE 1ST 2000

It seems that many people think I am retiring even though I have no such plans and did not once say so to anybody. Mirco Illic called today to say he read in *I.D.* that I am out of the design game – even though when I checked, the little article quite clearly stated that I am just dropping out to do a year without ~~clients~~.

I think there is so much dishonesty surrounding job changes (i.e. one 'quits' when one really got fired etc.) that many always assume the worst. If people who actually like me get it like this, I can only guess what the ones who hate my ass concoct. Well, so be it.

Then, of course, so far I have done exactly zero experimentation (initially there were some ~~client~~ projects to complete and now we are finishing up a book on the studio).

~~Clients~~ are still calling, trying every angle to get new projects accepted. When I say 'No, I am just doing experiments for the entire year', a popular approach is to present their projects as 'experiments'. On the other hand, I am of course flattered to be in such demand.

Set up on the roof alone for the first time this summer, read and wrote and watched the sun go down over New Jersey, this warm light stretching all the way uptown, the Empire State in all white (my absolutely favourite Empire colour) and thinking what a crime it is to have this crazy city and to not be taking it in and admiring it daily. Well, that for sure will change now. I am excited about the vacuum in front of me. Nothingness waiting to be filled. Wonderful.

Also finally had time to look at that Sol Lewitt catalogue I bought two month ago at the San Francisco MOMA. My favourite part is that he thinks its ok if anybody copies his wall drawings, he even sees that act as a complement and would regard the result, if the instructions are faithfully followed, as an original Sol Lewitt.

That is one glorious concept.

This could be a beautiful way out of my 'mediocre ideas=large distribution=huge cultural impact' and 'good ideas=small distribution= tiny cultural impact' dilemma. The dilemma that the mediocre coke can has enormous worldwide impact, while Walter DeMaria's 'Lightning Field' is reserved for the enjoyment of a few. It would be great to come up with the visual equivalent of the Linux computer operating system, a creative idea or system whose rules are published, but is improved and implemented by people around the world.

JUNE 2ND

We won best of show at the Design Biennial in Brno, Czech Republic and at the Warsaw poster competition.

At first I was excited about winning these two very respected long-running shows. But, then doubts came up: there is an entire group of highly talented, mostly European designers who create posters for the tiny theatres, rock concerts, or worst of all, environmental or peace posters.

With few exceptions, these things are printed in small runs of a couple of hundred, I guess only a couple of dozen of which actually go up in the street, the rest is distributed to various design competitions, museums, collectors around the world. It's just such a waste of talent that all this energy goes into the creation of something that nobody outside of the design community ever sees. We should be designing coke bottles, postal trucks and huge commercial web sites instead of leaving those jobs (which really do have cultural impact) to the marketing/branding idiots.

JUNE 26TH

What I do understand now is that the anger I sometimes have at ~~clients~~ was within me. It's my choice to get angry or not. I would have those angry urges in any profession. With no ~~clients~~ around to have bad thoughts about under the shower in the morning, I come up with substitute devils like bathtub re-glazers or roof fixers to be annoyed about. I hope to remember this silliness when I take on ~~clients~~ again.

If you want to get large things done you need the help of a lot of other people and you will encounter a certain amount of human politics. It's just an integral part of the game. I should expect a certain amount of politics and be ecstatic if it does not happen rather than disappointed when it does.

JUNE 30TH

Graphic design is a language. So, of course, I can go and learn another language, like film or music (the two that hold the biggest interest for me) and after some significant training I'll be able to speak them in a way that other people understand (and hopefully find interesting enough to watch and listen to). Or, instead of learning a new language, I can refine the one that I do know how to speak and, much more importantly, figure out if I actually have something to say. It would be hilarious to spend ten years learning how to direct a film only to find out I have nothing to say.

JULY 18TH

A couple of Swiss designers were in here yesterday; they said they had pictured me totally differently after having seen the Aiga Detroit poster. My soft and skinny self must have been disappointing. I always tell the story of how I wanted to portray anxiety and frustration (which is as much part of the daily design process as fun and creativity) in that poster, but if I'm honest, that really is an after-the-act explanation. The truth is, I had seen a Catherine Opie photograph of a woman with a children's drawing cut into her skin and did the 'Whereishere' piece a couple of months later.

By the time I did design the Detroit poster I had totally forgotten about the Opie photograph – when I saw it again I was shocked to discover how close they were. Of course, there are many other examples of visuals resembling mine. Actual type was cut into skin by Marilyn Manson fans and I'd wish I'd been influenced by that rather than by an artist. Stealing from life is ok; stealing from art is not.

JULY 19TH

I think there is one relatively untapped field in design: design that has a strong story behind its making. The success of the Detroit poster is surely based on it being actually carved as opposed to photo shopped (and therefore creates all the questions/stories about if I still have scars etc.). The granddaddy of this kind of design (or at least the first one I am aware of) is the Pink Floyd animals cover, where, on the insistence of the band (and against the will of its designers) they photographed that huge flying pig as an inflatable for real (instead of retouching it in) hovering above the Battersea power station in London. The ropes securing the pig broke and with the guys with guns to shoot it down on lunch break, the giant pig drifted all the way up to Wales, finally landing on the land of a rather freaked out farmer, the entire episode generating considerable press coverage.

We should be designing coke bottles, postal trucks and huge commercial web sites instead of leaving those jobs (which really do have cultural impact) to the marketing/branding idiots.

JULY 21ST

Made a little list of things I learned in my life:

1. Helping other people helps me.
2. Doing the gutsy thing always works out well.
3. Thinking that life will be better in the future is stupid, I have to live now.
4. Organizing a charity group is surprisingly easy.
5. Being not truthful always works against me.
6. Good and bad things I do always come back to me.
7. Assuming is stifling.
8. Drugs feel great in the beginning and become a drag later on.
9. Over time I get used to everything and start taking it for granted.
10. Money does not make me happy.
11. Travelling alone is helpful for a new perspective on life.
12. Keeping a diary supports personal development.
13. The need to look good limits my life.
14. Material luxuries are best enjoyed in small doses.

AUGUST 17TH

Proofread our book *Made You Look* again yesterday and even though I get tired of it I think it's as good as I can make it. There are so many experimental books by graphic designers out now that I just wanted to design a full show/tell book instead.

AUGUST 22ND

Thought of some furniture ideas incorporating paper. A stool is made out of a stack of paper on a yellow shipping crate; it's always clean and will bring you closer to earth over time. Pix: paper stool. The chair version could be made out of different hues of coloured paper. As you tear the top sheet off, the chair gets darker or lighter or cooler or hotter.

AUGUST 28TH

Smack into all this *The New York Times*, featured an article on Robert Rauschenberg. In it he states that he tries never to come into the studio with an idea. If he has an idea before starting, he goes for a walk just to get rid of that idea. He says if he does start with an idea, chances are he'll only come up with stuff that he or somebody else has done before him. He wants all the insecurities and doubts of the working process to become part of the final piece. This is so incredibly different from how I work. But I did try it today on the Anni catalogue and even though it was difficult to get started I have to admit it did yield some pages that were very different to what I've done before: I would have never thought of using that without the Rauschenberg method.

AUGUST 30TH

I have to find a way to use my time more efficiently; hours seem to fly by and I have not all that much to show for it in the evening. In two weeks I should probably start with my actual hourly plan just like in school, keep the breaks at certain times so I don't wind up doing the coffee-making/peeing/e-mail answering at all hours. It should also help me get back in charge of my time rather then always reacting to outside demands.

So I put a schedule together, tried it out and found it rather difficult to fulfil. When I finally counted the hours I realised I had put myself down for 64 hours per week. I redid a new one at 46 hours; this should be possible.

Monday morning 10:00-11:00 am: free thinking, 11:00-12:00 a big idea.

Afternoons contain easy things like Friday 4:00-6:00: going to galleries.

SEPTEMBER 1ST

I have to stop taking on any jobs at all. I let myself be talked into designing a clock for a World Studio charity auction, I am doing the Anni catalogue, I am probably redesigning the vans for the Coalition for the Homeless, I am so stupid, I wound up replacing my ~~clients~~ with pro-bono work. The studio feels exactly the same but now we don't get paid no more.

SEPTEMBER 2ND

Thought about jobs I would like to design once the studio is open again:
— A King Crimson CD cover.
— An electronic music (possibly Austrian) CD cover.
— The Coke can or something with similarly wide distribution (as long as something great is possible).
— A book of pure experimentation.
— A piece of web design that is so good that people will send it to each other.

SEPTEMBER 11TH

We had a First Tuesday meeting last week at Pushpin. These are monthly gatherings of around 15 New York design group heads discussing different subjects like 'Copyright' or 'How to hire great people.' The subject this time was 'me' (and my year without ~~clients~~). Everybody seemed mostly interested in how I manage it financially. Answer: own studio outright, no mortgage, saved some money in the good economy, kept studio small.

SEPTEMBER 19TH

I should start working seriously on my 'big project,' the one I was talking about when I realised how small I often dream and how my abilities, contacts and mentors would allow me to reach higher. I know I would have to do it based on teamwork, map the whole thing out, excite other people about the project, and most importantly, delegate. One thought came to my mind being stuck in Chicago O'Hare was an idea for an airport building in the shape of huge airplanes, thus giving the impression from the air that the actual planes are feeding of the large, plane-like buildings. Moms with their kittens.

SEPTEMBER 25TH

Sat in the lovely hot tub on top of my roof after working out yesterday: what an unbelievable feeling, probably the closest you can come to ecstasy without taking it. As I was sitting in total bliss I also thought about how the designer of this great device, the soft tub, is totally unknown. True, it is not particular good-looking but the joy it can give compared to the money spent is unbelievable. There are not many devices available for $2000 that can give that much joy (a used motorcycle or old convertible are the only ones that come close). If I compare that to my Droog design lamp that cost more and does absolutely nothing but light up the room in a pretty way, the benefits of high-end, famous design are tiny indeed.

OCTOBER 2ND

Just read an interesting and obvious idea in Eye: graphic designers are very much like actors, they work mostly from a given text that they have to interpret in their own way. Lets try which actor has an equivalent star in the design world:
Paul Rand = James Cagney
Tibor Kalman = Jack Nicholson
Paula Scher = Susan Sarandon
David Carson = Brad Pitt
Charles Spencer Anderson = Kevin Costner

OCTOBER 17TH

Came back from the AGI conference in beautiful Oaxaca, Mexico, a gorgeous colonial Spanish city surrounded by Aztec pyramids. It's strange to see all these gold-laden images in the churches looking so much like Russian icons, Italian Gothic and Greek Byzantine art: all that talk about global branding being a phenomenon of the 20th century is bullshit, the Catholics managed to pull this off 400 years ago.

NOVEMBER 15TH

Everybody still seems to be in love with graffiti. Most of it is just tags, the 'nick name' of the sprayer. Unlike in Europe where much of the spraying was for political reasons, in New York it all seems about self-promotion or worse, staking up ones territory. Peter Gerardi from Funny Garbage did a whole talk about his graffiti background at the Aiga National Conference in Las Vegas where he somewhat proudly mentioned that some people got killed because they sprayed over other peoples graffiti. What exactly is cool about that? Some idiot killing a person for ruining their self-promo?

JANUARY 8TH 2001

Read some more in the Bruce Mau book. It's a mixture of great original ideas, Tiborisms and overblown art speak. When designing the logotype for a book called 'Incorporations' he puts four different typefaces on top of each other to form a new fifth one. Only he writes he arrived at this by 'using strategies of addition, subtraction and superimposition, exploring the space between existing moments of typographic stability.' Hilarious.

Art speak is really no better then the similarly overblown corporate speak. They both come from the same motivation: instead of clarifying – for which they were invented – they wind up excluding. I also have a suspicion that both are used mostly by the more mediocre minds in their respective fields. At airports I hear middle managers forever droning on about 'contacts of sale' and 'proactive requisitions'. It's hard to imagine a Frank Gehry or a Jack Welch talking like that.

FEBRUARY 7TH

One of the more rewarding little experiments I've been conducting this year is the 'design of a fictitious CD cover including a 12 page booklet in three hours' exercise. I'm not trying to become more efficient but rather would like to see how the process and the results change when I only have three hours instead of our customary three months available. I'm doing them every Thursday from 9:00-12:00 and so far have been rather surprised by the results. A couple of directions I have never even thought of exploring came out of it.

MARCH 8TH

A little incident observed on my way to the TED Conference in Monterey. We all get out of a 30-seater plane from LA and advance to the tiny luggage pick-up. Quarks discoverer and Physics Nobel Prize winner Murray Gell-Man runs into a fellow Nobel Prize winner. Both carry exactly the same, cheap, freebie carry bags with the words 'World Economic Forum' printed on them. They nod in recognition and Murray asks: 'Isn't it sooo practical for travelling". It's amazing and sweet that after discovering the very nature of matter and winning a Nobel price there still is a need to show off as well as a need to pretend not to.

MARCH 14TH

Now I'm sitting in the business centre of the Hotel Nacional in Havana (talking about the need to show off), trying to get somebody to help me to get on the net. Cuba is wonderful. Stuck in the fifties, derelict and gorgeous, incredibly friendly people everywhere. The only stiff ones are the tourists (including me at times). But we saw practically no visual art to speak off, at least none readily available (not counting regular tourist souvenirs and some third-rate photo exhibits). I bought the only book on Cuban graphic design available, it's all good quality sixties work, much influenced by the Swiss school. The stuff you see on the streets is not even dreadful, just unremarkable non-design. It's strange that a revolution who promised to put art for the masses on the forefront of its agenda seem to produce so very little, while the mainstays of capitalism like the US, England and Japan control the visual art scene.

MARCH 30TH

About all that heart-touching stuff: it's easier to touch anybody if you have more time available to do so. That's why the really big movie dramas (*Gone with the Wind*, *Titanic* etc.) are 3 ½ hours long, why Art Spiegelman's great *Maus* comics was practically ignored when serialized in *Raw* and only took off published as a continuous narrative in book form. I, of course, have always preferred the novel to the short story. Is there ANY possibility to create a piece of design that involves the viewer more then five seconds? A CD cover containing much information? Well, that's not really touching. There is the graphic novel, of course. There would be lots of opportunity to create a new direction using digital photography and Photoshop. It's rather unbelievable how underemployed Photoshop really is in that sense.

APRIL 17TH

And then there is the interesting question where you do want to do something good:
In your family.
In your building.
In your immediate community, profession.
In your town.
In the world.

Edward DeBono divides them up in me-values (ego, status, pleasure, achievement etc), mates-values (acceptance in group, not letting the group down, etc), moral values (religious, general values of a particular culture) and mankind values (ecology, human rights etc). Quentin Crisp said at SVA that he never met a guy who did a lot of good for mankind who was not a total shit to all his friends. When I related this to Maira Kalman she mentioned her father who was a philanthropist but didn't know how to love his family.

MAY 13TH

I'm at the Typo in Berlin. This was definitely the starriest reception I've ever got. After hundreds of people already stood in line for my second talk on the medium stage, it had to be moved to the main one too. The on-site bookstore had 25 of our books, sold those, than ordered 50 more by UPS from the distributor, I signed them for people standing patiently in line, sold out, they ordered another 100, sold out the next day until they even got the whole contingent from the Fontshop too and sold these as well. They might have done many more. I think this book might actually be the one piece of our work that actually has impact; at least I remember how much of an influence Bob Gill's book *Forget All The Rules about Graphic Design (including the ones in this book)* had on me when I was a student. The question now is: What do I do with this? It is a fantastic situation to be in and there are a couple of things to watch out for:

1. The big head.
2. Not doing any work and resting on laurels.
3. Becoming unfocused.

JUNE 8TH

At yet another conference in San Francisco, feeling good in a wonderful room with a great view, cigar-smoking and coffee-drinking. Went out to the speakers' dinner last night where we played a little game at our table: everybody had to share a high and low point of the past week. Even though I was at the end of the table and had plenty of time to think about it, it was actually difficult to decide which high point I should use and I really did NOT manage to come up with a good low point. Must be doing something right.

My year without clients is over. It turned into 15 months – the first three were spent ~~finish~~ing up the book about our studio. Since this was not experimental time I quickly decided it won't count. In the remaining 12 months I worked mostly on concepts rather then complete projects, it just seemed to be a better way to spend my time.

I'll really know whether this sabbatical was worth my while two years down the line when I'll see if any of the exercises influences the work.

As I do look forward to actually get projects back from the printer again I also expect stress, so beautifully absent during the entire year, to hit me again. Getting anxious already.

Many warm greetings from
— Stefan